Officer Career Management

Additional Steps Toward Modernization

ALBERT A. ROBBERT, CAITLIN LEE, WILLIAM H. WAGGY II,
KATHERINE L. KIDDER, NATASHA LANDER, AGNES GEREBEN SCHAEFER

Prepared for the Office of the Secretary of Defense
Approved for public release; distribution unlimited

RAND NATIONAL DEFENSE RESEARCH INSTITUTE

For more information on this publication, visit www.rand.org/t/RR4337

Library of Congress Cataloging-in-Publication Data is available for this publication.
ISBN: 978-1-9774-0508-1

Published by the RAND Corporation, Santa Monica, Calif.

Cover: flickr.com.

Preface

The 2018 and 2019 National Defense Authorization Acts (NDAAs) (Public Laws 115-91 and 115-232) called for the Secretary of Defense, in consultation with the secretaries of the military departments, to provide a series of three reports on potential changes for regular and reserve officer career management, including some statutory changes enacted into law. The Director of Officer and Enlisted Personnel Management within the Office of the Secretary of Defense (OSD) asked the RAND National Defense Research Institute (NDRI) for assistance in obtaining perspectives from service secretariat, military, and reserve staffs on the issues covered in these reports. Findings were published in a report titled *Officer Career Management: Steps Toward Modernization in the 2018 and 2019 National Defense Authorization Acts* (Robbert et al., 2019).

Work on these issues led policymakers within the OSD to identify other potentially useful steps toward modernization of officer career management. The RAND NDRI was again asked to evaluate these potential steps and to obtain the perspectives of the military departments where appropriate. This report provides findings from that effort, which was completed in calendar year 2019. (A series of appendixes with additional information is available as a separate online volume [Robbert et al., 2021].) Since the potential steps we evaluated in this effort were complementary to the momentum generated by the 2018 and 2019 NDAAs, we titled this report so as to indicate the linkage. The research reported here was completed in March 2020 and underwent security review with the sponsor and the Defense Office of Prepublication and Security Review before public release.

This research was sponsored by the OSD and conducted within the Forces and Resources Policy Center of the RAND National Security Research Division (NSRD), which operates the National Defense Research Institute (NDRI), a federally funded research and development center sponsored by the OSD, the Joint Staff, the Unified Combatant Commands, the Navy, the Marine Corps, the defense agencies, and the defense intelligence enterprise.

For more information on the RAND Forces and Resources Policy Center, see www.rand.org/nsrd/frp or contact the director (contact information is provided on the webpage).

Contents

Figures

Tables

Summary

In previous research, the Director of Officer and Enlisted Personnel Management (OEPM) within the Office of the Secretary of Defense (OSD) asked the RAND National Defense Research Institute (NDRI) to assist in obtaining perspectives from the military departments and services on the issues covered in reports required by the 2018 and 2019 National Defense Authorization Acts (NDAAs) (Robbert et al., 2019). The research underlying this document built on that work by exploring a series of related issues identified by officials within OSD. Specifically, NDRI was asked to determine any statutory, policy, cultural, or fiscal constraints on the military departments' flexibilities regarding those issues, to gather service perspectives on the issues, and to offer potential mitigation strategies for any apparent constraints. The issues identified for this research are grouped by topic in Table S.1.

Table S.1. Issues for Analysis, Grouped by Topic

Promotions	
	Could technical-track competitive categories have requirements-based promotions in lieu of "up or out"?
	What statutory changes are required to allow different competitive category promotion boards to have different promotion rates and frequencies?
	Could the Department of Defense (DoD) establish policies to ensure officers who opt out of promotion consideration during the early years of implementation are not adversely affected at future statutory boards?
	Could DoD advocate a return to permanent and temporary promotions?
	Could DoD recommend selection board guidance regarding deployability?
Tenure	
	Could promotion boards have more liberal show-cause provisions to account for stagnant officers? What are the limits of the current provisions in this regard?
	Given the legislative change removing the requirement to achieve 20 years of commissioned service by age 62, what controls, if any, could be put in place?
	What statutory and policy changes are required for officers to be contracted the way that enlisted members are today and what are the pros and cons of doing so?
Other Issues	
	Given a common retirement system for active and reserve personnel and the anticipated alignment of benefits under the duty-status reform initiative, what is still missing to provide for continuum of service/permeability (switching components at will)?
	What legislation is necessary for all services to have warrant officers (WOs) and limited duty officers (LDOs)?
	Could an "officers without rank" concept provide additional flexibility for technical and traditional officer career tracks (e.g., medical, legal, cyber, acquisition, or others)?

Methodology

We leveraged a combination of qualitative and quantitative methods to analyze the eleven issues in Table S.1. Qualitative assessments drew on relevant aspects of the Defense Officer Personnel Management Act (DOPMA) and the Reserve Officer Personnel Management Act (ROPMA), relevant Department of Defense Instructions (DoDIs), studies conducted by RAND and other research organizations, and professional and academic journal articles and books. We used this initial literature review to develop a baseline understanding of limitations on officer management flexibilities and to create a framework for assessing those constraints along four dimensions: statutory, policy, cultural, and fiscal. We also conducted additional quantitative analysis when the literature or stakeholder suggestions raised research questions that allowed for modeling with readily accessible Defense Manpower Data Center (DMDC) data. We then engaged in stakeholder discussions with both internal RAND officer management experts and with current policymakers, including principals and other representatives from OSD, service secretariat, and military staffs responsible for officer management policy, to confirm or disconfirm our findings.

Change in Complex Systems

As a foundation for this work, we first sought to understand why the recent wave of officer management modernization changes has proceeded with little of the pushback encountered by similar but much more comprehensive Force of the Future (FOTF) proposals that were introduced in 2015 (Carson, 2018). We found well-documented rationales for incremental rather than comprehensive adaptation of change in complex bureaucratic systems. It is difficult to predict the full effects and interactions of comprehensive change in complex systems or even to understand, retrospectively, the impacts of individual elements of change. Evaluating change is especially difficult in military organizations, because the impacts that matter the most are fully observed only in wartime, and there is a risk that changes introduced in peacetime may not work in wartime. Incremental change provides a means to drive down that risk.

Constraints on Additional Change

We found that the most prevalent constraints on potential officer modernization thrusts are cultural. Culture tends to limit adaptation of change in all eleven of the issues we examined. There were only very limited statutory, policy, or fiscal constraints observed for the range of changes explored in the three promotion issues. Statutory, policy, and fiscal constraints were much more commonly observed in the tenure and other issues we examined.

Service Perspectives

To characterize service perspectives, we identified three ways that the services seem to be reacting favorably regarding an issue: routinely using available statutory or policy provisions, open to experimenting with available provisions, or seeking new statutory provisions. We also identified two ways that services might be reacting negatively to some of the issues: little or no interest in available provisions or little or no interest in seeking new provisions implied by the issue. Our findings are summarized in Table S.2.

Table S.2. Categorizing Issues by Availability and Use of Statutory and Policy Provisions

Issue	Available Provisions Sufficient and Routinely Used	Services Open to Experimentation	Services Seek New Provisions	Little or No Interest in Available Provisions	Little or No Interest in New Provisions
Promotions					
Requirements-based promotions for technical-track competitive categories		X			
Differentiating promotion rates and frequencies across competitive categories	X	X			
Opting out of promotion consideration		X			
Reserve commissions for active duty officers as an aid to active/reserve component permeability[a]					X
Promotion board guidance regarding deployability	X				
Tenure					
More liberal provisions for stagnant officers			X		
Commissioning age controls					X
Contracted service for officers					X
Other					
Additional enhancements for active/reserve permeability		X	X		
WOs and LDOs in all services	X (Navy and Marine Corps)			X (Air Force—WO)	X (Army—LDO, Air Force—WO and LDO)
Officers without rank					X

[a] The original issue, a return to temporary and permanent promotions, is reframed here in terms of the sponsor's interest in the use of reserve commissions for active duty officers as an aid to active/reserve component permeability.

The services were open to experimentation with available flexibilities in all three promotion-related issues. Although no specific implementation plan was identified, several of the services mentioned interest in using alternative promotion authority, with its expanded promotion zone, to match promotion considerations to the development and utilization patterns suitable for highly technical fields. The Navy differentiates promotion rates and frequencies for its line officers to a greater extent than the other services; the Air Force and the Marine Corps are the least differentiated, but the Air Force has recently announced a split of its line officer competitive categories, which could possibly lead to more differentiation of promotion outcomes. All the services are contemplating opt-out policies; the Army recently published a governing regulation in that regard.

Among the tenure-related issues we examined, only the need for better tools to prune stagnant officers stood out as requiring new provisions. Although not ideal for this purpose, the services, particularly the Navy, use force-shaping authorities to involuntarily retire officers who detract from or no longer contribute effectively to service objectives. While our analysis suggests that stagnant-officer issues are very limited, we found that more flexible authorities would be useful.

Despite much discussion and effort devoted to removing them, impediments to movement between active and reserve components remain significant enough to discourage full utilization of available human capital to meet defense needs. Statutory changes, such as duty-status reform, have removed some impediments, and the services have developed workarounds for others, but much more could be done to enhance permeability between the components.

The Way Forward

For OSD and the services, the way forward would encompass two of the five categories shown in Table S.2—those in which the services are open to experimentation or seek new provisions. For the four issues in which the services are open to new experimentation—namely, requirements-based promotions for technical-track competitive categories; differentiating promotion rates and frequencies across competitive categories; opting out of promotion consideration; and additional enhancements for active/reserve permeability—the services could be encouraged to experiment with new flexibilities, always subject to the discretion of the service secretary regarding how far and fast to pursue them. For the two issues in which new provisions seem warranted and sought after by the services—more liberal provisions for stagnant officers and additional enhancements for active/reserve permeability—OSD and the services could begin or continue dialogue on legislative proposals to provide new flexibilities.

Acknowledgments

The authors would like to express gratitude to all the experts in officer management across the military services and the DoD who graciously offered their time and insights to this project. Our research also benefited immensely from many informative conversations with Michael Melillo and Matthew Phillips of the office of the Deputy Assistant Secretary of Defense for Military Personnel Policy, and our sponsor, Lernes J. Hebert, who served as the deputy assistant secretary during the course of our project.

We also thank John Winkler, who provided thoughtful input on the scope and substance of the document, and Amanda Kraus and Peter Schirmer, who offered thorough and constructive reviews. And finally, we thank our production editor, Amanda Wilson, for assistance in polishing the final report.

Abbreviations

AC	active component
ADF	Australian Defence Force
AGR	Active Guard Reserve
APZ	above the promotion zone
AVF	all-volunteer force
BPZ	below the promotion zone
BRS	Blended Retirement System
CP	continuation pay
CSL	centralized selection list
DMDC	Defense Manpower Data Center
DoD	Department of Defense
DoDI	Department of Defense Instruction
DOPMA	Defense Officer Personnel Management Act
eSERB	enhanced selective early retirement board
FOTF	Force of the Future
FTS	full-time support
FY	fiscal year
GNA	Goldwater-Nichols Act
GS	General Schedule
IDES	Integrated Disability Evaluation System
IPPS	integrated pay and personnel system
IPZ	in the promotion zone
LDO	limited duty officer
MPA	Military Personnel Appropriations
NDAA	National Defense Authorization Act
NDRI	National Defense Research Institute

OCS	Officer Candidate School
OEPM	Officer and Enlisted Personnel Management
OSD	Office of the Secretary of Defense
PCS	permanent change of station
RC	reserve component
ROPMA	Reserve Officer Personnel Management Act
ROTC	Reserve Officer Training Corps
RPA	Reserve Personnel Appropriations
SERB	selective early retirement board
SES	Senior Executive Service
TDY	temporary duty
TFAP	Total Force Assignment Program
TIG	time-in-grade
UCMJ	Uniform Code of Military Justice
U.S.C.	United States Code
WO	warrant officer

1. Introduction

A series of provisions in the 2018 and 2019 National Defense Authorization Acts (NDAAs) (Public Laws 115-91 and 115-232) has precipitated a fresh look at the statutory and policy framework for military officer career management. These provisions pertain to portions of Title 10, United States Code (U.S.C.), commonly referred to as the Defense Officer Personnel Management Act (DOPMA) and the Reserve Officer Personnel Management Act (ROPMA). The NDAAs called for the Secretary of Defense, in consultation with the secretaries of the military departments, to provide a series of three reports on an extensive list of potential changes.

Some changes were adopted in the 2019 NDAA. These included repeal of the requirement to be able to complete 20 years of service by age 62 upon commissioning, broadened authorities for use of constructive service credit, extension of temporary promotion authority to all military departments (previously authorized only for the Navy), optional merit-based promotion list sequencing, provisions for officers to "opt out" of promotion consideration, lowering the grade threshold to O-3 (it was previously O-5) for eligibility to continue to 40 years of service, and an alternative promotion authority featuring a more flexible promotion timing framework.

In previous research, the Director of Officer and Enlisted Personnel Management (OEPM) within the Office of the Secretary of Defense (OSD) asked the RAND National Defense Research Institute (NDRI) to assist in obtaining perspectives from the military departments and services on the issues covered in the three reports required by the NDAAs (Robbert et al., 2019). While deliberating these issues, officials within OSD identified a series of eleven issues related to modernization of officer career management that they believed warranted investigation. To capitalize on the depth its staff had developed in assisting with the NDAA reporting requirements, the Director of OEPM asked NDRI to examine the additional issues. Specifically, NDRI was asked to determine any statutory, policy, cultural, or fiscal constraints on the military departments' flexibilities regarding those issues, to gather service perspectives on the issues, and to offer potential mitigation strategies for any apparent constraints.

To aid in conducting our qualitative and quantitative analyses, we grouped most of the eleven issues raised by OSD into two bins: promotions and tenure. Three issues fell outside of these bins: additional flexibilities for technical or professional tracks, statutory provisions regarding warrant officers (WOs) and limited duty officers (LDOs), and active/reserve permeability. The issues, grouped this way, are listed in Table 1.1.

This report provides the findings developed by NDRI regarding these issues. It provides information of interest to legislators, legislative staffs, and defense, military departments, and military service officials contemplating changes in officer management statutes or policy. As readers will note, some but not all of the eleven issues pertain to new officer management provisions included in the 2019 NDAA.

Table 1.1. Issues for Analysis, Grouped by Topic

Promotions

Could technical-track competitive categories have requirements-based promotions in lieu of "up or out"?

What statutory changes are required to allow different competitive category promotion boards to have different promotion rates and frequencies?

Could the Department of Defense (DoD) establish policies to ensure officers who opt out of promotion consideration during the early years of implementation are not adversely affected at future statutory boards?

Could DoD advocate a return to permanent and temporary promotions?

Could DoD recommend selection board guidance regarding deployability?

Tenure

Could promotion boards have more liberal show cause provisions to account for stagnant officers? What are the limits of the current provisions in this regard?

Given the legislative change removing the requirement to achieve 20 years of commissioned service by age 62, what controls, if any, could be put in place?

What statutory and policy changes are required for officers to be contracted the way that enlisted members are today and what are the pros and cons of doing so?

Other Issues

Given a common retirement system for active and reserve personnel and the anticipated alignment of benefits under the duty-status reform initiative, what is still missing to provide for continuum of service/permeability (switching components at will)?

What legislation is necessary for all services to have WOs and LDOs?

Could an "officers without rank" concept provide additional flexibility for technical and traditional officer career tracks (e.g., medical, legal, cyber, acquisition, or others)?

Background

DOPMA, enacted in 1980 as Public Law 96-513, modified or changed substantial portions of Title 10 pertaining to active officer personnel management. ROPMA, enacted in 1994 as part of the NDAA for fiscal year (FY) 1995 (Public Law 103-337), changed similar portions of Title 10 pertaining to reserve officers. Since their enactment, the provisions of these laws have been subject to continuing analysis, review, and revision, but their major features have remained intact. These include

- a closed system in which, with few exceptions, officers enter at low grades and higher grades are filled through internal promotion
- a pyramidal structure for the field grades (O-4 through O-6) relative to each other and to the company grades (O-1 through O-3) collectively, formed by grade ceilings tables based on total officer strength in each of the services
- a competitive, up-or-out career flow maintained by established high years of tenure for various grades and requirements that officers twice nonselected for promotion are subject to involuntary separation
- seniority-based promotion timing, including time-in-grade (TIG) requirements for promotion, defined zones of promotion consideration based on date of rank, and promotion lists sequenced by date of rank

- uniformity across services, with statutory provisions authorizing or directing the Secretary of Defense to prescribe uniform regulations for implementation (Parcell and Kraus, 2010).

Statutory changes adopted in the 2019 NDAA provided measured departures from these characteristics. Expanded authority to award constructive service credit can make lateral entries (accession of officers above the entry grade of O-1) more attractive. Alternative promotion authority, opting out of promotion consideration, and merit-based promotion list sequencing allow greater differentiation of promotion timing and opportunity across segments of the officer force. These changes create opportunities to move segments of the officer force into a career management structure that is less closed and less lockstep than the traditional DOPMA/ROPMA framework.

The tone of the portions of the 2018 and 2019 NDAAs that are applicable to officer management suggests that enactment of additional statutory flexibilities is possible and that they will be shaped through ongoing dialogue among the armed service committees, their staffs, OSD, military department, and military service staffs. This report is intended to help advance that dialogue

Methodology

Our findings were based on a mix of qualitative and quantitative research. We began the project with a qualitative assessment of the existing professional and academic literature on the officer management areas of interest identified for this study. The review included relevant aspects of DOPMA and ROPMA, relevant Department of Defense Instructions (DoDIs), studies conducted by RAND and other research organizations, and professional and academic journal articles and books. We used this initial literature review to develop a baseline understanding of limitations on officer management flexibilities and to create a framework for assessing those constraints along four dimensions: statutory, policy, cultural, and fiscal. We also conducted additional quantitative analysis when the literature or stakeholder suggestions raised research questions that allowed for modeling with readily accessible Defense Manpower Data Center (DMDC) data. We then engaged in stakeholder discussion with current policymakers, including principals and other representatives from OSD, service secretariat, and military staffs responsible for officer management policy, to confirm or disconfirm our findings.

Some of these discussions occurred in a series of officer management modernization roundtables organized by OEPM with participation by service secretariat and military staff representatives and members of our RAND research team. Others occurred in separate meetings with each service's representatives. Service representation at those meetings included core policy experts who participated in the OEPM roundtables. As a final step in obtaining service perspectives, these same representatives reviewed a draft of our report and corrected any misstatements. We also consulted with internal RAND officer management experts to enhance our understanding of constraints on officer management flexibilities.

Organization of the Report

Chapter 2 provides a discussion of officer management reform in its broader historical context. Chapters 3 and 4 cover the issues contained within our promotion and tenure bins in Table 1.1. Chapter 5 covers the remaining three issues. In Chapters 3 through 5, we provide a brief statement of the motivation for examining each issue, followed by a table summarizing any statutory, policy, cultural, or fiscal constraints on the military departments' latitude to address the issue and their available mitigation strategies. When appropriate, we expand on the table contents and, in some cases, provide other useful material pertinent to the topic. Chapter 6 provides our conclusions and recommendations. A series of appendixes with additional information is available as a separate online volume (Robbert et al., 2021).

2. "Muddling Through": The Revolutionary Potential of Evolutionary Officer Management Reform

The FY 2019 NDAA reforms provided a springboard for the military services to pursue innovation in the officer management system. To ensure these initial flexibilities and future reforms are implemented effectively, it will be important for stakeholders, including Congress, OSD, and the services, to identify the factors that lead to innovation success and failure in the officer management system.

The history of officer management reform suggests that bureaucratic politics plays a central role. Organizations seek to maximize their expected utility—that is, power, prestige, and resources—while at the same time minimizing uncertainty by adopting routine processes that reinforce shared values and accepted facts (Allison and Halperin, 1974; Allison and Zelikow, 1999). This is particularly true for military organizations, which perform inherently high-risk missions in highly uncertain threat environments (Murray, 1996, p. 24; Rosen, 1991, pp. 8, 69–71). As a result of this desire to adhere to accepted processes, innovation in military organizations often occurs incrementally; in other words, military organizations have extra incentives to "muddle through" change, rather than adopting comprehensive changes quickly.[1]

The purpose of this chapter is to identify the costs and benefits of the incremental approach and to examine its implications for stakeholders pursuing innovation in officer management. Of course, senior defense officials or lawmakers could choose to initiate change without regard for bureaucratic preferences for incrementalism. But as discussed below, historical cases of officer management reform do not suggest that this is an effective strategy. Rather, past cases indicate innovators make progress when they embrace incrementalism as a means to pursue effective change.

This chapter provides a discussion of two contrasting attempts at officer management reform: DoD's Force of the Future (FOTF) initiative and the subsequent reforms enacted in the FY 2019 NDAA. It then discusses the differences between comprehensive and incremental change and the reasons why military organizations in particular might prefer incremental change, and then builds on that explanation with additional historical examples. Finally, the chapter closes with some thoughts on the implications of incrementalism for officer management reform in the future.

---

[1] Lindblom (1959, 1979) first used the phrase "muddling through" in organizational change studies. See discussion later in this chapter.

Historical Background: The Rise and Fall of the Force of the Future

In 2015, then–Secretary of Defense Ashton Carter announced FOTF, a series of initiatives designed to transform DoD personnel management. The officer management system was a main target of the reform. Brad Carson, the acting Under Secretary of Defense for Personnel and Readiness at the time, called for a series of new initiatives centered on an internal labor market that matched up individual talent and military requirements (Carson, 2018).

The proposals, which Carson billed as "the biggest personnel overhaul in 45 years," marked a sharp break with the "up-or-out" officer management framework codified in the 1980 DOPMA (Carson, 2015; Sisk, 2016). That system focuses on time-driven promotion consideration for cohorts of officers, based in part on successful completion of key career developmental assignments. Applying largely to active-duty officers, it puts a premium on the promotion of officers with the skills required to lead large numbers of forces into battle (Misztal, Rametta, and Farrell, 2018). The system is designed to remove officers who are twice passed over for promotion, thereby maintaining a steady flow of officers into mid- to senior grades. To date, it has evolved only slowly, building on not just DOPMA, but a variety of laws, policies, incentives, history, and culture that constitute the officer management system writ large.

Carson and other FOTF advocates argued that the existing framework is outdated because it emphasizes developing officers for industrial-era wars, rather than creative, entrepreneurial officers well-positioned to manage competition and conflict in an increasingly dynamic and complex threat environment (Tilghman, 2016). But the spate of reforms underlying FOTF drew criticism from lawmakers, their staffs, and senior uniformed leaders, who disagreed that the existing system is broken and questioned whether fundamental change was necessary (Matthews, 2015; Maucione, 2016, 2017).

However, less than three years later, after the departures of both Carter and Carson, several new officer management flexibilities became law in the FY 2019 NDAA. Since then, as described in the remainder of this report, a renewed interest in officer management reform has begun to percolate across DoD and the military departments, which are now exploring the potential use of the FY 2019 flexibilities and seeking to better understand the degree of existing latitude that already exists across legal, policy, and cultural fronts.

Change Success and Failure: The Role of Bureaucratic Politics

Why did the military services embrace the FY 2019 NDAA reforms after rejecting FOTF? One explanation is that FOTF lacked support from uniformed military leaders. Some experts speculated that FOTF failed because those leaders did not want to break with the officer management practices that had effectively singled them out for promotion to the highest ranks (Cancian and Harrison, 2015). Other experts noted that uniformed military leaders were reluctant to embrace reforms that had been pushed on them by senior civilian DoD leadership, rather than developing organically within the military services to meet specific warfighting needs (Carter et al., 2017).

These explanations expose the darker side of bureaucratic politics, in which bureaucracies may resist change when it does not conform to cultural preferences favoring the status quo. This resistance is not necessarily rational, and, in fact, it can be detrimental to progress within an organization. While cultural blinders can certainly play a central role in thwarting productive change—countless innovation studies document this phenomenon (see, for example, Adamsky, 2010; Kier, 1997; Lee, 2016)—there is also a less cynical dimension to bureaucratic politics that helps to explain why bureaucracies might resist change: the pragmatic need to move slowly and incrementally as a means to drive down risk.

Types of Bureaucratic Change

Incremental change involves taking small steps through a process of "successive limited comparisons": policymakers adjust a policy, compare outcomes of the new policy with the status quo to measure relative success, and then repeat this process as new data emerges and goals change (Lindblom, 1959, pp. 80–81). Also known as "muddling through" (Lindblom, 1959) or "sustaining change" (Christenson and Overdorf, 2000), incrementalism is the dominant approach to innovation in large organizations because comprehensive change is often either not possible or inadvisable due to inability to foresee its consequences; organizational insights typically build on each other in a linear fashion, leading to policy change by small steps (Lindblom, 1979, p. 517). DoD's historical approach to officer management reform has typically followed this incremental, or evolutionary, pattern of reform (Rostker et al., 1993, pp. 1–2).

Although large bureaucracies such as DoD tend to adopt incrementalism, sometimes they can move beyond it. When innovative insights reach a critical mass, they can produce a *paradigm shift*, or a revolutionary change, which is completed when incremental changes are understood in a new light that allows old ways of thinking about a problem to be replaced with a completely new one (Kuhn, 1962).

In contrast to these two change mechanisms, Lindblom cites a theoretical ideal—rarely if ever achievable in the context of real-world policymaking—known as *comprehensive change*. This change mechanism applies a more formal, theoretical approach to deal with a policy problem all at once, in a holistic manner. First, the desired outcome is identified, in isolation from existing policies; next, every factor that could possibly impact that outcome is considered; and finally, the success of the policy is measured based on whether the means are achieving the desired ends. In practice, comprehensive change differs from incremental change because it involves dealing with policy as an integrated whole and conducting a complete and scientific analysis of policy alternatives (Lindblom, 1979, p. 517).

Any kind of change has the potential to lead to military innovation, which can be defined as "a change in operational praxis that produces a significant increase in military effectiveness as measured by battlefield results" (Grissom, 2006). As discussed below, military innovation in the officer management system is difficult to measure in war and even harder to measure in peacetime, yet the impact of an innovation on battlespace performance remains the gold standard for measuring the effectiveness of military personnel reforms.

Incremental Change, Paradigm Shifts, and Comprehensive Change in Military Organizations

Organizations may resort to incremental change at least in part because it is impossible to know everything about a problem. Give the "bounded rationality" of organizations, which operate based only information available (Simon, 1957), it becomes necessary to tackle *parts* of problems, rather than the whole, to minimize the possibility of making ill-informed judgments that lead to innovation failure (Lindblom, 1979, p. 518). In the absence of complete information, it is difficult to effectively execute a comprehensive change all at once. Additionally, with multiple, interacting changes implemented simultaneously, it is difficult to predict beforehand or ascertain retrospectively the partial impacts of the individual elements of change.

Incrementalism, with its focus on only a subset of a particular problem, allows organizations to gather the information they need to make only stepwise changes to the status quo and measure their relative effectiveness. Incrementalism also limits the potential for unanticipated second- and third-order effects because the change is limited in scope, reducing the odds that its impact will be outsized or that it will interact with other changes in unexpected ways.

Incrementalism may prove particularly attractive to military organizations, because the strategic environment is riddled with uncertainty (Freedman, 2013, p. xi). Organizational theory posits that large organizations will seek to *minimize* this uncertainty—rather than confront it head on—through the development of standard operating procedures, routine ways of doing business that become so embedded in an organization that they become second nature (Allison and Zelikow, 1999, pp. 168–171). Change of any type is therefore not only difficult, but inherently problematic because it cuts against deeply engrained mechanisms designed to keep the organization functioning smoothly. Change may be even more difficult for federal bureaucracies, which may be more committed to procedures that have proven successful in the past as a means to ensure continued financial support from Congress and the White House (Wilson, 1989, p. 221).

But change is arguably *most* difficult for military organizations, compared with others. Military institutions face more uncertainty than other organizations because they do not fulfill their warfighting function in peacetime; it is therefore difficult to judge the merit of existing organizations and procedures until the test of battle—let alone the merit of alternative ones (Murray, 1996, p. 24; Rosen, 1991, pp. 8, 69–71). Whereas private-sector organizations might be able to test new ideas in particular market segments, military institutions can rely only on imperfect wargames, simulations, and modeling to predict if new policies will achieve their organizational aim: fighting and winning wars. Furthermore, the stakes are higher for military institutions, which perform tasks in environments with at least the potential for violence.

Commanders may prefer to rely on standard ways of doing business based on the principle that these organizational structures, weapons systems, strategies, operations, or tactics are "tried and true" and therefore less likely to put lives at risk (Nielson, 2003, p. 15).

For military organizations, aiming for incremental change provides a means to drive down risks. Most importantly, a standard exists for measuring the effectiveness of incremental change: its impact relative to the status quo. In contrast, comprehensive changes may be so dramatic that there are no good measures of effectiveness outside of a wartime test. In peacetime, these innovations may, at best, appear to be proverbial "solutions in search of a problem," until they can be proven in the crucible of battle. At worst, they may generate unanticipated second- and third-order impacts, not all of them positive. And even in wartime, it may be difficult to isolate the importance of any one particular change in the officer management system—incremental or comprehensive—relative to the myriad other factors that shape battlespace outcomes. This point leads naturally to the next, which is that incremental change provides a means not only to assess the change during relative peacetime (against the status quo) and minimize the risk of unintended consequences, but also to assess its impact in wartime with less risk; because the change breaks off only one part of a problem, the impact of failure on the battlefield is minimized.

The Pros and Cons of Incrementalism: A Review of Some Historical Examples

While incrementalism does not immediately lend itself to comprehensive change, its cumulative impact can lead to significant innovations (Lundvall, 1992). The U.S. government's decision to switch from selective service to an all-volunteer force (AVF) is an example of a military innovation involving a series of incremental insights that ultimately led to incremental change, and, finally, a paradigm shift. The emergence of the AVF began with the accretion of new information over a period of years, which established the foundational evidence required for a wholesale shift in thinking. The old paradigm of selective service, which lasted from 1948 to 1973, fell under growing scrutiny in the early 1960s for a variety of reasons, including perceptions that deferments had spiraled out of control, that a draft system was at odds with a free society, that men should not have to serve in the unpopular Vietnam War, and that discipline problems among conscripts in Vietnam were mounting (Rostker, 2006, pp. 2–4).

The new paradigm, which espoused a return to the American tradition of voluntary service, began to emerge at the same time that the disciplines of sociology and economics began to make increasingly meaningful contributions to the study of military manpower. The intellectual revolution bred a series of studies, most notably the work conducted by the Gates Commission, which provided the scientific evidence to support a move away from conscription. Upon reflection, it perhaps was not surprising that the evidence pointed to this conclusion: A large proportion of military accessions was already voluntary, in keeping with the American tradition of avoiding conscription (Rostker, 2006, p. 19). Still, it was this analysis, conducted over a period of years, that created the momentum for the services, Congress, and the White House to support the birth of AVF in 1973 (Rostker, 2006, p. 137). While early critics questioned whether

AVF was a successful military innovation—arguing that such a force might not be willing to fight—the subsequent success of the 1984 Panama invasion and the outcome of Operation Desert Storm demonstrated that AVF led to the fielding of "arguably the finest military force the United States had ever sent into battle" (Rostker, 2006, pp. 532–533).

Another notable example of incrementalism leading to a paradigm shift in officer management, as well as a significant military innovation, is the Goldwater-Nichols Act (GNA) of 1986. Built on the National Security Act of 1947, GNA offered a spate of reforms to improve "jointness," including joint education and training requirements for any officer seeking promotion to the rank of general or flag officer.

The legislation itself took more than four years to pass, due to the military services' reluctance to embrace the reform, which subsumed much of their former power under the Chairman of the Joint Chiefs of Staff and the combatant commands (Locher, 1996). In addition, the services also shared a rational concern that the legislation would put significant additional burdens on officers to fulfill joint requirements (Levine, 2019). The concern remains a live issue today (Levine, 2019), with outside experts noting that officers must cram an additional four or five years of joint-related assignments on top of a full career (see, for example, Rostker, 2015). In this light, the services' early resistance to GNA, which could have been at least partially motivated by a parochial interest in maintaining power, also seems to reflect a genuine concern about moving too fast on GNA because of its impact on the efficacy of the officer management system.

When GNA eventually became law with the support of Congress and the White House, it effectively led to a paradigmatic shift in officer management by mandating joint-duty positions, establishing Joint Specialty Officers, making promotion to flag rank dependent on joint experience, and, critically, empowering the Chairman of the Joint Chiefs of Staff to achieve successful implementation (Miller, 2001, p. 289).[2] Although the concerns of the officer corps probably contributed to a delay in GNA enactment, the delay also presented an opportunity to refine the legislation through analysis and study (most notably by the blue-ribbon Packard Commission). And in the end, the law was widely viewed as effective, emphasizing a greater joint focus that contributed to the successful outcome of the U.S. military–led Operation Desert Storm in 1991 (McInniss, 2016, pp. 8–9; Miller, 2001, p. 289).

In contrast to these incremental cases, it is difficult to identify a case of successful officer management reform that was *not* incremental for all the reasons previously identified. That is not to say that incrementalism is entirely without downsides. In 1980, the President signed into law DOPMA, which codified the previous patchwork of policies governing military officers and updated numerical constraints on field grade officers (O-4–O-6) in each service. Ten years after

---

[2] White House and Congressional support was bolstered by the Packard Commission, which produced a series of studies in favor of reform.

it was enacted, a retrospective review indicated that while the law introduced some reforms, such as permanent sliding grade scale tables, a single promotion system, and elimination of regular and reserve distinctions within the active-duty officer force, it essentially amounts to a static description of existing practices and lacks the levers or flexibility to accommodate changing officer management requirements (Rostker et al., 1993, pp. v–vi).

Even when incrementalism does lead to a paradigm shift, stakeholders may still have to satisfice, accepting that incrementalism is not ideal but may be the only option for a large military bureaucracy. The pace of incremental change can be less than ideal, and in the absence of visionaries who see the potential for revolutionary change, the fruits of incremental insights and changes can be ignored. During World War II, for example, the U.S. Navy relieved 30 percent of its overly cautious submarine commanders for cause in 1943, replacing them with younger, more aggressive commanders willing to take the risk required to surface their subs in order to attack Japanese merchant ships (Rosen, 1991, p. 131). Yet while the personnel replacement was seen as highly successful at the operational level, there was no commensurate strategic shift in the Navy to systematically target merchant shipping as an effective means to destroy Japan's economy (Rosen, 1991, pp. 143–147). Measures of effectiveness to assess the impact of the sub attacks on the Japanese economy emerged only after the war, when it became clear that the campaign against the Japanese economy, of which the sub attacks were a large part, had come close to breaking the empire (Rosen, 1991, pp. 143–144).

In this case, comprehensive change would have been beneficial. The desired outcome—breaking the Japanese economy—would have been a clear strategic goal from the outset, and the variables impacting that outcome, including the actions of the submarine force, would have been carefully evaluated. Measures of effectiveness—in this case, the number of Japanese ships sunk by submarines—would have been recorded and linked to this outcome. In practice, however, gaining an essentially omniscient understanding of such a complex problem from the outset was not possible. And even today, despite the emergence of ever-increasing computing power, it is still difficult to comprehensively understand and resolve complex policy problems in such a systematic manner.

As described in Table 2.1, the more typical pathway to innovation, even in the presence of a pressing threat, is incrementalism, which mitigates risk by reducing uncertainty about change. It focuses policymakers on a particular part of a problem for which the information is knowable, or mostly knowable, and for which some standard of effectiveness (the status quo) already exists against which the outcome of the change can be measured. And in a best case, when a new strategic goal becomes clear, that incremental change can lead to a paradigm shift like the one the U.S. military experienced with the advent of the AVF and GNA.

Table 2.1. Incremental Versus Comprehensive Change

Change Mechanism	Level of Uncertainty	Measures of Effectiveness	Innovation Potential	Personnel Reform Example
Incremental	Low to medium • fixed number of variables to consider • desired outcome clear	Measured in terms of improvement over the status quo	Can lead to innovation, but builds on effective changes and insights over time	Shift to the AVF
Comprehensive	High • large number of variables to consider • desired outcomes less clear	No clear measures of effectiveness for individual elements of change	May create momentum for innovation, but may lack evidence of effective change and insights to support change	Original FOTF proposal

Change in the Officer Management System: Lessons Learned from the Force of the Future

FOTF advocates sought to model their movement on AVF (Carson, 2015; Kane, 2011), but in practice the reform effort was dissimilar. Rather than seeking an incremental accrual of insight and smaller changes made over time, FOTF advocates argued for a comprehensive overhaul (Carson, 2015; Kane, 2011; Vandergriff, 2015). For example, in his book *Bleeding Talent*, Tim Kane, a leading supporter of FOTF, lamented what he saw as the large numbers of talented personnel leaving military service due to a "deeply anti-entrepreneurial personnel structure" that does not reward merit. He called for the wholesale replacement of the current personnel system with an internal job market that would "create a new web of incentives rewarding creative leadership" (Kane, 2011). Members of the Defense Entrepreneurs Forum, a nonprofit focused on "bottom-up" innovation, similarly advocated for a "holistic" approach to personnel reform (Defense Entrepreneurs Forum, 2018). FOTF advocates called to stanch the bleeding of talent (see, for example, Bensahel and Barno, 2015), with a shift toward market principles to better recruit and retain said talent (Carson, 2015).

The proposals, which Carson billed as "the biggest personnel overhaul in 45 years," initially centered on the elimination of the existing "up-or-out" system in favor of approaches rooted in market principles and "talent management" (Carson, 2015; Sisk, 2016). The second and third tranches of the FOTF proposals focused on military parents and flexibilities to improve retention of exceptional military and civilian personnel (Iyengar et al., 2017). Although some of the FOTF initiatives, in and of themselves, had been well-researched and garnered some level of support, taken together they appeared to be too much for lawmakers, who questioned the wholesale shift to a "corporate" approach to officer management (Sisk, 2016), potentially high costs, and a lack of evidence to support some of the key initiatives (Iyengar et al., 2017).

In response to congressional criticism, Carson eventually scaled down FOTF, proposing the following reforms in November 2015 (Bensahel and Barno, 2015):

- more "on-ramps" so more civilians can enter service later in their careers
- short-term "off-ramps" to allow military personnel to gain new experience outside the military and then bring an innovative outlook back into the force
- harnessing big data to track trends and create talent management platforms to better match military personnel with available positions
- conducting exit surveys to better understand why people leave service.

Among some experts, the reforms were portrayed as "watered down" or low-hanging fruit," falling short of FOTF's initial objective to replace "up or out" with a market-driven talent management system (Bensahel and Barno, 2015; Cancian and Harrison, 2015). In practice, however, these reforms represented a pragmatic recognition that changing the system overnight would be difficult to do. The more modest goals generally sought to increase flexibility in the existing officer management system, relative to the status quo. In a piece written after FOTF faltered, Carson acknowledged the difficulty of pushing comprehensive change through a bureaucracy but credited the original sweeping proposals with generating previously lacking momentum for personnel reform (Carson, 2018).

But the gambit yielded mixed results. The administration's initial presentation of FOTF as comprehensive reform still remained fixed in the consciousness of lawmakers, who continued to reject the reforms when Carson testified on Capitol Hill in January 2016 (Shane, 2016). Because FOTF was proposed in this manner, support still hinged on answering the difficult questions that comprehensive change almost inevitably raises. Although Carson ultimately introduced reforms that were arguably incremental in nature—some of them, such as on-ramps and off-ramps, appeared in the FY 2019 NDAA reforms—FOTF advocates were stuck defending a comprehensive approach that required (1) articulating a clear vision of how FOTF would increase battlespace effectiveness; (2) demonstrating an understanding of costs and other second- and third-order effects; and (3) providing clear measures of effectiveness.

In the end, Carson's decision to seek comprehensive change played a role in the failure of FOTF to gain purchase among the military departments and U.S. lawmakers. Bureaucratic politics had a significant hand in this turn of events. Critics pointed out that cultural biases among military leaders—including a preference to control and preserve the officer management system that had led to their own promotions—played a role. But the initial FOTF push for comprehensive change also cut against more pragmatic considerations preoccupying both lawmakers and uniformed military members. These stakeholders readily identified the complexity and risk associated with the looming, existential questions implicit in a comprehensive approach. While Carson and other FOTF advocates may have recognized that true comprehensive change was not possible, it appears they may not have anticipated the degree of backlash to a proposal for comprehensive change, which appeared to mute any momentum it created. Even when the reforms were scaled down, the accusation that the reform had become "solutions in search of a problem" remained (Maucione, 2016).

The alternative to the comprehensive approach to officer management reforms is to continue on a path of incremental change, and to do so in a way that is transparent and systematic so that the costs and benefits of the changes can be analyzed and addressed. Of course, making small changes relative to the status quo implicitly supports, at least in the near term, the continuation of the current officer management framework: an "up or out" promotion system that measures success in terms of preserving a "pyramid" with many junior officers at the bottom and far fewer senior ones at the top.

As reform advocates have noted, that system, fundamentally designed to breed commanders with the physical strength and leadership skills required to command large field armies, may not be ideal for technology-infused and dynamic twenty-first-century warfare. In the future, battlespace effectiveness may well depend on officers with different sets of skills and attributes, such as technological savvy, creative thinking, and the ability to rapidly innovate. Yet in order to move the officer corps closer to this ideal, continuing an incremental approach that builds on decades of existing insights on officer management reform appears to present the most practical way forward.

The Future of Officer Management Reform: Continuing the Evolutionary Approach

In 2018, Carson argued that the passage of the FY 2019 reforms marked a vindication of FOTF, because even though they are not comprehensive, the reforms were enough to spur a paradigm shift in personnel management (Carson, 2018). Others argued that the 2018 National Defense Strategy, which called for the "broad revision of talent management among the Armed Services" provided the impetus for what they characterized as the most significant legislative change since the enactment of DOPMA (Misztal, Rametta, and Farrell, 2018).

Yet the FY 2019 reforms are far from a paradigm shift or even a "broad revision." Rather, they grant significant flexibility to the military departments to implement changes at the pace and scope they judge to be most appropriate, or to avoid the reforms altogether. Furthermore, none of the proposed reforms reflects a philosophical shift in thinking; rather, they show a willingness to build on incremental insights of the past to gain additional insights and make more changes, which, in turn, could *eventually* lead to a paradigm shift in thinking about officer management.

At the same time, the relatively incremental nature of these reforms does not negate the danger of going too far, too soon. As OSD and the military services consider the implications of the new legislation for the existing officer management system, they can draw important lessons from the FOTF experience. None of the FY 2019 reforms propose shifts as comprehensive as the original FOTF proposal, but they do allow for the services to scale the change to varying degrees. In the following example, the alternative promotion authority in the FY 2019 NDAA shows how an overly broad implementation of a reform, or a decision to implement more than one reform in the same population, can increase complexity to the point that it becomes difficult to predict outcomes.

Calibrating Reform: The Alternative Promotion Authority

One of the most potentially expansive reforms in the FY 2019 legislation is the new alternative promotion authority. The purpose of the authority is to give the military departments more flexibility to determine the timing of individual officers' promotions. DOPMA provided service secretaries the authority to vary the timing and promotion opportunity among competitive categories in order to meet service needs. Alternative promotion authority allows for similar differentiation among officers within a designated competitive category without the stigma of failure within a narrowly defined promotion zone. The utility of this new authority is that it gives the services a chance to experiment with moving away from time-driven promotions.

The Mechanics of the Alternative Promotion Authority

The alternative promotion authority allows the service secretaries to designate one or more competitive categories for which standard tenure management considerations do not apply. First, the new legislation allows for a wider promotion window. Under current DOPMA provisions, for each promotion board a new cohort of officers is defined by date of rank to be *in the promotion zone* (IPZ). If not selected from this cohort, they compete for future promotions *above the promotion zone* (APZ). Additionally, some highly qualified officers may be selected *below the promotion zone* (BPZ); that is, before reaching the promotion zone. Under the alternative promotion authority, however, there are no BPZ or APZ promotions. Second, under current DOPMA provisions, officers twice passed over for promotion to grades O-4 or O-5 (after one IPZ and one APZ consideration) are subject to being separated or retired (if eligible) from active duty unless selected for continuation through a board process or removed from the reserve active-status list. But under the new legislation, officers can be considered for promotion up to five times before being considered for selective continuation; the military departments have the discretion to determine the timing and number of promotion opportunities for officers in the alternative promotion authority category (Robbert, et al., 2019, pp. 78–79).

In effect, the alternative promotion authority allows officers to stay in their grades for much longer or shorter times than would be typical under existing tenure management rules. However, the service secretaries do have to provide to Congress an explanation of the number of promotion considerations to be afforded, an estimate of promotion timing within the category, and an estimate of the size of the promotion zone.

Conversations about the alternative promotion authority are often tied to discussions of career fields that require deep technical expertise, such as flying aircraft, conducting cyberspace operations, or developing artificial intelligence systems. In these fields, some argue that officers may benefit from longer time in grade, allowing them to spend more time honing their craft rather than stepping through a mix of command and other assignments at fixed intervals. Yet while the alternative promotion authority is often tied to technical tracks, it does not have to be. The legislation can be applied to any officer subpopulation, or even to an entire officer population, should a service secretary choose to leverage the authority in that manner.

An Expansive Approach to the Alternative Promotion Authority

If a service secretary were to apply the alternative promotion authority across a substantial swath, or even the entire officer population, doing so might raise several of the earlier problems identified in association with comprehensive change. While the desired outcome might be clear—perhaps the purpose would be to increase flexibility in officer careers to improve retention—the change would introduce considerable complexity, and therefore raise the level of uncertainty and make predicting how it would impact motivation and retention of officers at various levels of talent and accomplishment difficult. One of the biggest uncertainties concerns the question of milestones. Because the alternative promotion authority breaks with time-driven promotions, it would seem important to develop new milestones to determine promotion timing. But milestone-based promotions raise a variety of issues, which would become fairly numerous and complex if the alternative promotion authority were widely applied across the officer population.

- **Determining milestone achievement:** Identifying the point at which an officer had achieved a particular set of milestones, whether they were competencies or experiences or something else, could be difficult. Officers might achieve milestones to greater or lesser degrees, so the milestones might need to be weighted and tracked at the individual level.
- **Administrative burden:** The services might face a greater administrative burden in having to track these individual milestone achievements across the officer corps.
- **Potential loss of hierarchical structure:** If a milestone approach allowed individuals to promote at different paces, as opposed to in a cohort, it might be difficult or even impossible to maintain the existing pyramid structure.
- **Less systematic flexibility:** Once officers are moved into the alternative promotion authority, it would be difficult to move them out. The service would be committed to giving them a fixed number of promotion considerations prior to their being considered for selective continuation.
- **Race to the bottom:** If the services did manage to develop a relatively uniform milestone approach that allowed for promotions by cohort, they might then see a "race to the bottom," as career field managers compete to lower the milestone standards in their career fields to allow quick promotion relative to other career fields (Robbert et al., 2017, Table 2.1 and p. 9).
- **Unpredictable interactions with other reforms:** If the alternative promotion authority was employed simultaneously with other reforms—lateral entry, for example—the impact on the grade structure, as well as other second- and third-order effects, would be even more difficult to predict.

An Incremental Approach to the Alternative Promotion Authority

In contrast to this expansive approach, the services have shown more interest to date in cautiously exploring the use of the alternative promotion authority as a means to deepen expertise in technical career fields (Robbert et al., 2019, pp. 27–29). To the extent that they have expressed interest in it, they have tended to view it as a discrete measure that would be implemented on a relatively small scale, independently of other reforms.[3] This more incremental approach eliminates altogether two of the issues mentioned in a more expansive approach—namely, the potential for a race to the bottom and unpredictable interactions with other reforms. By scaling the effort to focus on a small officer population, the services can also likely reduce, although perhaps not eliminate, the impact of the other issues cited above. The incremental approach would give them the analytical space and time to address these and other issues if they did arise, while preserving the functionality of the current officer management system for most promotions. In contrast, the more expansive approach would put the whole system at risk, with no quick or easy way to back out of the change.

Conclusion

Recognizing that the military departments are beginning to show some appetite for new officer management flexibilities, OSD asked RAND to consider legislative, policy, fiscal, or financial limits on various reforms. But another important consideration is the extent to which policymakers may want to self-impose limits on the scale and timing of reforms to ensure that desired outcomes, measures of effectiveness, and results of the changes can be clearly identified, documented, and effectively leveraged over time.

Historically, the U.S. military has pursued an incremental approach to officer management reform to ensure the continued predictability and stability of the existing officer management structure. The discussion in this chapter suggests that an incremental approach, which scales the reforms to small populations (at least initially) and avoids implementation of more than one reform at a time, could, over time, add considerable flexibility to that system. Somewhat ironically, an incremental approach that largely preserves the existing system, but allows for the accumulation of smaller changes and insights over time, appears to be the most realistic way to eventually establish a new twenty-first-century system that breaks with many of the principles of officer management as they exist today.

---

[3] Discussion with U.S. Army, U.S. Navy, U.S. Marine Corps, and U.S. Air Force representatives, August 2019.

3. Promotions

This chapter discusses the five issues related to various aspects of officer promotion management:

- Could technical-track competitive categories have requirements-based promotions in lieu of "up or out"?
- What statutory changes are required to allow different competitive category promotion boards to have differing promotion rates and frequencies?
- Could DoD establish policies to ensure officers who "opt out" of promotion consideration during the early years of implementation are not adversely affected at future statutory boards?
- Could DoD advocate a return to permanent and temporary promotions?
- Could DoD recommend selection board guidance regarding deployability?

Issue: Could Technical-Track Competitive Categories Have Requirements-Based Promotions in Lieu of "Up or Out"?

The purpose of establishing a technical-track competitive category is to enhance the career development and retention of officers in career fields where technical qualifications, often gained through extensive education, training, or experience, weigh more heavily than in conventional military occupations. One notional example is the creation of a "fly-only" track in the Air Force to support pilot retention goals (Robbert et al., 2018, p. 7). Costly developed human capital can be lost unnecessarily if traditional DOPMA-compliant promotion opportunities and up-or-out policies are applied to management of officers considered to be on a technical track. In this issue, we explore options for avoiding such losses.

In this context, *requirements-based* refers to the concept of promoting and retaining technical-track officers to meet explicit service needs for higher-grade or longer-tenured officers with technical qualifications, providing very high promotion opportunity to avoid "up or out" losses while accepting slower promotion tempos that might be required to balance inventory with requirements, and not necessarily seeking to mold the inventory into a conventional pyramid-shaped grade distribution. *Requirements-based* might also imply promoting officers only after they have met specific developmental milestones or when assigned to positions authorized at higher than their permanent grade. Table 3.1 summarizes constraints that would arise in pursuing any of these options.

Constraints

Service secretaries have the authority to set the timing and opportunity for promotions under either conventional or alternative promotion authorities, based on the needs of the

Table 3.1. Requirements-Based Promotions for Technical-Track Competitive Categories

Domain	Constraints? Yes	Constraints? No	Comments	Mitigation Strategy
Statutory				
Timing/ opportunity		X	Service secretaries can set timing and opportunity in technical-track competitive categories to approximate fully qualified selection (see 10 U.S.C. 623 regarding establishment of promotion zones), but selection rate will be limited to 95 percent per provision in pending FY 2020 NDAA.	
Milestones	X		Current statute supports the use of time-driven requirements, but not milestone-driven requirements. Per 10 U.S.C. 619(c)(1), each officer in a promotion zone must be considered.	Use secretarial board guidance to stress the importance of milestones. Alternative promotion authority would better accommodate this approach. Consider legislative proposal to allow for milestone-driven requirements.
Temporary promotions		X	Authorized per 10 U.S.C. 605 when occupying position higher than permanent grade. Must be in a skill with a critical shortage of personnel and must be approved by a board convened for this purpose.	
Policy		X	Under a milestone approach, military departments would have to track progress at the individual level.	
Cultural	X		Timing/opportunity approach would likely result in considerably slower promotions for technical-track competitive categories.	Socialize slower promotions as an expected feature of technical-track career paths.
Fiscal		X	Could have negative retention impacts, but fiscal impact might be favorable if reduced force costs are less than increased training costs.	

service.[1] Existing selection processes and opportunity rates for medical doctors and dentists have some characteristics of a technical-track promotion concept—opportunities constructed to avoid up-or-out losses. One emerging concept of a technical track for line officers envisions part of a conventional career field branching off into a track where expectations for developing technical competencies are higher than normal and for developing broader leadership and management competencies are lower. To avoid up-or-out losses, promotion opportunity can be set at high levels, but to avoid too great an allocation of DOPMA-grade ceilings to such competitive

[1] Alternative promotion authority, a statutory provision provided in the 2019 NDAA, allows for a wider promotion window and modified up-or-out provisions (see 10 U.S.C. 649a).

categories, promotion tempo can be slower than that of conventional line competitive categories.[2]

If *requirements* pertain to developmental milestones, alternative promotion authority, as authorized in the FY 2019 NDAA, would better accommodate the issue. Officers are likely to vary in the career points at which milestones are met. Alternative promotion authority would provide the needed variation in promotion timing to allow it to coincide with the expected variation in meeting milestones.

Statutory authority for temporary promotions, previously provided only for the Navy, was extended to all services in the FY 2019 NDAA. One provision of the legislation allows its application only when the service secretary determines that there is a critical shortage of personnel in the officer's skill. If a shortage in the officer's full career ladder is needed as a prerequisite for use of this authority, it would limit its utility in addressing higher-grade shortages in a skill with good overall manning (e.g., with company-grade overages that offset field-grade shortages). However, the Navy—the only service with experience with this authority—has interpreted the requirement to be satisfied if the shortage is in a grade/skill combination.

Overall, as Table 3.1 indicates, there are relatively few constraints on the adoption of various approaches to requirements-based promotions for technical tracks, aside for some cultural adjustments to slower promotions. However, a strictly milestone-based promotion eligibility approach or a temporary promotion mechanism in the absence of a skill shortage would lie outside of current statutory constraints.

With regard to implementing requirements-based promotions and several other issues, we saw the potential for a negative retention impact. Whenever there is a retention impact, there is a potential fiscal impact also. Lower retention results in reduced force costs because the lower-retention force has a lower years-of-service profile (to which pay and allowances are tied), and a lower proportion of the force earns retirement benefits. Lower retention also increases accession requirements and hence increases initial training costs. With the exception of specialties with very high initial training costs (pilots are one of the few examples), reductions in retention yield reduced force costs that more than offset increased training costs. Thus, without controlling for productivity, lower retention is generally less expensive. Accordingly, in this and other issues, we do not see reduced retention as a cause of encountering a fiscal constraint.

Service Perspectives

While some nonline competitive categories have long been managed using promotion policies with the characteristics of a technical track, as of this writing no service has

---

[2] 10 U.S.C. 523 establishes ceilings for field-grade officers as a function of the total number of commissioned officers serving on active duty. Section 595 of the FY 2020 NDAA (Public Law 116-48) requires a report on the history of service compliance with grade ceilings and an assessment of alternatives, including substituting annual grade authorizations in place of the current statutory grade tables.

implemented the approach for a line officer competitive category. However, we heard indications that some of the services are weighing the merits of testing the concept.

Proposed Way Forward

While no statutory changes are necessarily needed, DoD promotion policies could be revised to more explicitly recognize the likely emergence of technical-track competitive categories and to provide general guidelines for managing them. Since promotion zones are defined by TIG for both conventional and alternative promotion authority, we do not believe that service secretaries could premise promotion eligibility on meeting designated milestones. However, secretarial guidance to promotion boards could address the importance of designated milestones.

If a military department decided to adopt a milestone-based system, an incremental approach might be most appropriate, given the complexities described in Chapter 2. Secretarial guidance could be issued to allow officers to be included in a competitive category designated for alternative promotion authority only after meeting specified milestones. If the military department found that this approach yielded desirable results, the department could then offer a legislative proposal amending Title 10 to allow for milestone-based eligibility criteria in promotion considerations.

Issue: What Statutory Changes Are Required to Allow Different Competitive Category Promotion Boards to Have Different Promotion Rates and Frequencies?

DOPMA was intended in part to foster stable and predictable promotion outcomes. This is evident in the statutory requirement for service secretaries to size promotion zones such that officers would have "relatively similar opportunity for promotion" over a five-year period (10 U.S.C. 623). Because of language such as this, there may be perceptions that DOPMA requires such consistency across competitive categories. However, as summarized in Table 3.2, this is not the case.

Constraints

From a statutory perspective, DOPMA's requirement for consistency in promotion opportunity applies *within* rather than *across* competitive categories. This requirement appears in the context of a subsection that makes it applicable to a specific grade and competitive category. An accompanying provision explicitly requires service secretaries to consider the differing requirements of the various competitive categories when setting promotion quotas (10 U.S.C. 622).

Table 3.2. Promotion Rates and Frequencies Across Competitive Categories

Domain	Constraints? Yes	Constraints? No	Comments	Mitigation Strategy
Statutory		X	10 U.S.C. 623 requires sizing promotion zones to provide "relatively similar opportunity for promotion" over a five-year period; context indicates that this applies to a specific grade and competitive category. 10 U.S.C. 622 requires consideration of differing requirements of the various competitive categories when setting promotion quotas.	
Policy		X	Consistent with Title 10: "Promotion opportunity and timing, as determined by the Secretary of the Military Department concerned, may vary based on needs" (DoDI 1320.14, 2019, p.18).	
Cultural	X		Navy and, to a lesser extent, Army already employ multiple line competitive categories and therefore are more amenable to promotion timing and opportunity differentiated across career fields.	Air Force now implementing multiple line competitive categories—a path to potentially greater differentiation. Marine Corps also considering multiple line competitive categories.
Fiscal		X		

DoD policy reaffirms these principles:

> Promotion opportunity and timing, as determined by the Secretary of the Military Department concerned, may vary based on needs. It is desirable that the promotion opportunity and timing of officers serving on the ADL be consistent with the guidelines included in the enclosure of Reference (e). For Reserve Component officers, promotions are based on force requirements. The Secretary of the Military Department concerned will determine the timing and opportunity variables for promotion. (DoDI 1320.14, 2019, p. 18)

A close reading of DoD law and policy also suggests that, while promotion timing and opportunity need to be *relatively* similar over a five-year period, there could be some variation, even within the same competitive category and grade. DoDI 1320.13, 2014 (p. 6) provides a table indicating desirable promotion timing and opportunity, which signals a preference for consistency across competitive categories, but also clearly notes that service secretaries may diverge from the targets based on needs. As the services begin to experiment with technical-track promotion categories and alternative promotion authority (10 U.S.C. 649a–k), these targets will cease to be applicable. Alternative promotion authority is intended to provide greater flexibility in promotion timing. Also, since it will include multiple year-group cohorts in a promotion zone, promotion opportunity rates will be lower than with conventional promotion authority, which typically includes an approximately one-year group cohort in a promotion zone.

Service Practices

Understandably, some services might strive, for the sake of camaraderie, a sense of fairness, and esprit de corps, to maintain relatively consistent promotion outcomes across competitive categories. However, service secretaries clearly retain the discretion to ordain different outcomes as necessary to meet requirements. We note that the Navy, with multiple line officer competitive categories, differentiates timing and opportunity among them. The Army achieves a similar effect by setting career-field floors for promotion selections (given sufficient fully qualified officers among those competing for promotion). The Air Force has recently decided to move toward splitting its line competitive category, providing a potential path toward greater differentiation.

Proposed Way Forward

We do not see a need for statutory or policy changes. Service secretaries have the authority required to differentiate promotion timing and opportunity to meet the needs of their services.

Issue: Could the Department of Defense Establish Policies to Ensure Officers Who Opt Out of Promotion Consideration During the Early Years of Implementation Are Not Adversely Affected at Future Statutory Boards?

The FY 2019 NDAA included a provision that gives service secretaries the authority to allow officers to delay promotion consideration, otherwise known as *opt out*. The purpose of the opt-out program is to provide officers with incentives to pursue career broadening assignments, advanced education, or another assignment while on active duty, on the condition that the service secretary designates these activities—while not associated with the standard promotion milestones—as ones that will enhance the officers' ability to contribute to the needs of the service. Table 3.3 provides our key findings regarding this issue.

Constraints

We examined constraints to DoD's ability to implement an opt-out policy. As indicated in Table 3.3, the military services broadly possess the statutory authority to both pursue an opt-out policy and issue promotion board guidance. DoD policy clearly requires the services to issue promotion board guidance regarding the opt-out population, but several issues remain unresolved. The most significant challenges to implementation will involve cultural and fiscal factors, both in the type of officer who would be interested in opting out and on the ways in which officers could be adversely impacted by a decision to opt out. We address each type of constraint—statutory, policy, culture, and fiscal—in the subsections below.

Table 3.3. Opting Out of Promotion Consideration

Domain	Constraints? Yes	Constraints? No	Comments	Mitigation Strategy
Statutory		X	10 U.S.C. 615 permits board guidance.	
Policy		X	Current DoDI 1320.14 (2019) instructs service secretaries to issue board guidance that protects against adverse implications from a decision to opt out.	Several unknown aspects of opt out need to be addressed in policy: • Application on annual basis? • More than one consideration? • Timeliness of application? • Minimum standard of performance file quality? • Only certain broadening assignments?
			Perceived potential for officers to abuse opt out if not carefully managed.	Develop policies that set standards for meeting the opt-out criteria:
	X		Analysis indicates opt out participant might face discrimination in three ways: • direct discrimination from board • through performance reports • through different assignments.	• Consider tying long broadening assignments to opt-out consideration when appropriate. • Consider using analytical techniques to gauge whether officers who opt out face discrimination in promotion board proceedings. • In some circumstances, consider the use of a separate competitive category for promotion consideration.
Cultural	X		Implementation of opt out may send wrong signal regarding education and broadening assignments.	Set standards that limit opt-out candidates to high performers.
Fiscal		X	Could increase longevity, and thus cost, of some officers, but not in numbers large enough to impinge on a fiscal constraint.	

Statutory

10 U.S.C. 619 requires that the service secretary approve a request to opt out, that the action must be in the best interest of the service, and that the officer has not previously failed of selection for promotion. Eligibility to opt out is limited to officers in two categories: those who are "complet[ing] a broadening assignment, advanced education, [or] another assignment of significant value to the Department"; and those whose "career progression requirement [is] delayed by the assignment or education."

The statute does not further define what precisely a broadening assignment entails or how to determine if the assignment provides significant value to DoD; nor does the statute explain what is meant by a career progression requirement. The military services presumably possess wide latitude to define those terms within a reasonable context. For example, the U.S. Marine Corps is considering an opt-out option for specific aviators, which would allow them to opt out of promotion to remain in the cockpit to gain more experience after a long training pipeline. Such a policy might increase promotion opportunity for those specific aviators while also alleviating a company-grade pilot shortage.

10 U.S.C. 615 provides that the secretary of the military department can submit to the members of a promotion board "guidelines as may be necessary to enable the board to properly perform its functions." Using that authority, the military services can instruct board members to fairly and impartially consider those who delayed promotion consideration through the opt-out policy.

Policy

In March 2019, OSD updated its promotion policy to note that officers who opt out of promotion boards should be protected from any adverse implications when they are considered for future promotions (DoDI 1320.14, 2019). The policy states that secretaries of the military departments should prescribe instructions to promotion board members that they will not consider an officer's previous decision to opt out when the officer is considered for future promotions. However, to date, OSD and the military departments have not provided a clear indication of, how, exactly, they will prevent the board from considering the decision to opt out.

As a new provision yet to be fully implemented in policy, it has several areas that remain to be defined, including

- Will officers be permitted to opt out more than once per grade?
- Will officers be permitted to opt out for more than one year in a single application?
- How far in advance can/must an officer apply for opt out?
- Will officers be required to possess a minimum set of quality markers to qualify for opt out?
- Will only particular broadening assignments be considered for opt out?

Given that opt out is initiated by the individual, not the service, another policy concern among the services is the potential abuse of opt out if qualifications for the program were not tightly controlled by the service secretary (Robbert et al., 2018, p. 26). Early indications suggest that the services will tightly control the policy. For example, the Army, in establishing its opt-out policy, uses a series of approvals—from the individual to the first O-6 in the chain of command to the commanding general of Human Resources Command and finally to the Assistant Secretary of the Army for Manpower and Reserve Affairs—to validate an opt-out request. The Army defined three justifications for an opt-out request: "need to accept or complete an assignment of significant value to the Army"; "must complete an ongoing funded resident advanced civilian education program"; or "must complete a career progression requirement . . . that is delayed by either a priority assignment or the civilian education" (Department of the Army, 2019, p. 2). In addition, eligibility will be further limited to those who have not previously failed of selection for promotion or have derogatory information in their performance file in the current grade (U.S. Army Human Resources Command, 2019).

The Navy's approach differs from the Army's. Navy requests for opt-out consideration will be reviewed "a panel of, at a minimum, an Officer Community Management Branch URL [unrestricted line] community manager, a Navy Personnel Command Career Management Branch officer detailer, and one additional officer, all senior to the officer requesting to defer PSB [promotion selection board] consideration" (Department of the Navy, 2019a). After its review, the panel will forward its decision to the Assistant Secretary of the Navy for Manpower and Reserve Affairs.

Cultural

The most obvious and overt factor leading to adverse consequences for the opt-out population would be discrimination on the part of selection boards. By discrimination, we do not mean unethical actions or a failure to adhere to the responsibilities of a board member. Rather, we mean that all else held equal, selection board members may prefer individuals who did not opt out of a promotion board to those that did. Career timelines are different, potentially resulting in different promotion outcomes; this preference may not even be deliberate. Selection boards prefer officers crafted in the board members' image (Janowitz, 1971, p. 148). For those who have pursued traditional career timelines and milestones, nonstandard career paths might appear unattractive. The opt-out population might fit such a nonstandard mold, less because of an abnormal date of rank and more because of the atypical assignment that led to the opt-out consideration in the first place.

DoD policy addresses this form of discrimination by overtly targeting board member perceptions of those who opt out. The military services might struggle, however, to gauge the effectiveness of its board guidance. For instance, imagine that an officer opts out of a promotion board to complete graduate school before promotion to the next rank. If that officer is not selected by a future selection board, how can the military service tell that overt discrimination occurred? The officer, even with the opt-out protection, might still be missing traditional performance evaluations compared with his or her peers. The officer might have had a lower quality performance record prior to graduate school. The board members might discriminate against graduate school attendance, preferring other broadening experiences to formal education. With many confounding variables, some of which cannot be measured, analysis of promotion outcomes will be required to ascertain the future effectiveness of this policy.

Even if the rating chain inherently supports a decision to opt out, the rating chain might still adversely affect an officer pursuing opt out. Some services use a forced distribution numerical system in performance reviews, mathematically restricting the most favorable ratings. Officers are more probabilistically likely to receive a high-quality performance review immediately prior to a promotion board, with descending probability as the officer becomes more removed from consideration (Evans and Bae, 2017). An opt-out decision changes the date of the next promotion consideration. If an officer opts out of promotion consideration for one year, the next performance review might not be the final performance review before the selection board. The next performance review becomes the second from final, with a decreased probability that it is a high-quality evaluation.

The human resource bureaucracies employed by the military services align officers to their next assignment. Some assignments will better prepare individuals for the competition of a promotion board than other assignments, in ways that reflect traditional appreciations for the scope of responsibility, the prestige of the position or unit, or the alignment with an expected career path. If the assignment bureaucracies subsequently align individuals who use an opt-out provision to less advantageous assignments, a promotion board might incorporate the less-advantageous assignment into its decision, irrespective of the opt-out participation. If assignment bureaucracies discriminate against those who participate in opt out, the ramifications might manifest in promotion board decisions.

Another potential cultural implication of opt out relates to signaling. This concern, voiced by a representative in the Army, is that the implementation of an opt-out program for officers pursuing education—a PhD program, for example—sends the message that the traditional promotion system does not reward education and that therefore a workaround is necessary.

Proposed Way Forward

Military departments who choose to leverage opt out need to develop clear policies that specify the timing and qualification criteria for opting out. Several service representatives noted that the service secretaries need to retain flexibility to selectively determine a specific pool of officers who could opt out and need to set policy rules that would dictate the circumstances and duration under which an officer could opt out (Robbert et al., 2018, p. 26). While we were researching this policy issue, both the Army and Navy published their first opt-out policies. The Marine Corps, in addition, is considering policies to allow initially small pools of officers in specific career fields to opt out.[3]

Military departments may also want to consider establishing a high bar for opt out. Related to the issue of establishing opt-out standards, military departments may want to target the opt-out program toward exceptional performers interested in education and broadening assignments to mitigate any stigma. The Navy, for example, requires a review of "the documented performance history of the officer and ability to provide future benefit to the Navy," which might limit the opt-out pool to officers who would be highly competitive for promotion, but may need more time to meet key milestones as judged by assignment officers and branch heads (Department of the Navy, 2019a). The challenge, however, is ensuring a degree of fairness and transparency to any such high bar. If two officers with identical career timelines and broadening assignments differ only in the quality of their performance file, differing treatment of opt-out requests might be viewed as favoritism.

---

[3] Discussion with U.S. Marine Corps representatives, September 11, 2019.

Another consideration might be tying long broadening assignments, and in particular voluntary assignments that require service member applications, to opt-out consideration when appropriate. For officers interested in long broadening assignments, such as doctoral programs or extended fellowships, opt out increases the pool of potentially eligible applicants. By explicitly linking an application to opt-out consideration, the military services can remove uncertainty regarding whether an opt-out request would be approved. Such a process could go so far as approving a request to opt out at the same time as an approval for participation in a broadening assignment or program. Some officers who could not "fit" a long broadening assignment in their career timeline might do so under opt out. Linking a long broadening assignment to opt-out consideration in the same application process might be an efficient way of employing this flexibility. Officers who might not otherwise be eligible (or at a minimum ideal) for a long broadening assignment become better fits, while the service can choose from a larger pool of applicants and allow the officer to complete the broadening at a lower, and thus cheaper, rank.

To gauge whether officers who opt out face discrimination in promotion board proceedings, the services could leverage analytical techniques. Statistical analytical techniques could assist the military services in understanding if officers who use the opt-out provision face adverse outcomes. One such technique, propensity score–weighted doubly robust regression, was used by Nelson Lim and colleagues (2014) to evaluate whether women and racial minorities face discrimination in promotion board proceedings. The analysis estimates the difference in promotion outcomes between two groups who are similar, differing only in the variable of interest (race or gender, in their analysis). The technique could be applied to the opt-out policy, comparing those who opt out with those that did not.

Finally, in some circumstances, the services may wish to consider the use of a separate competitive category for promotion consideration, as required by Title 10 U.S.C. 621, whereby officers within a competitive category compete for promotion. In the most common use, a competitive category divides officers by career field, but this need not be its only use. Officers who have completed long broadening assignments, such as doctoral programs, could comprise a competitive category that contains officers regardless of whether they used the opt-out policy.[4] However, officers who complete long broadening assignments might be more likely to use the opt-out policy than officers who completed short broadening assignments. If promotion outcomes for those officers are a concern, separating them into their own competitive category could be an option. At the same time, a military service should consider modeling potential promotion outcomes to avoid scenarios where these highly broadened officers, by competing only against each other for promotion, eventually promote at a lower rate than if they had competed in a larger peer group.

[4] An officer could be in the competitive category for a portion of a career or the remainder of a career, depending on how eligibility for the competitive category is structured by the military service.

Other Considerations

Officers who opt out of promotion consideration might be ineligible later for involuntary separation due to failure of selection. 10 U.S.C. 632 provides that O-3s and O-4s who twice fail of selection to the next grade and are not eligible to retire will be involuntarily separated "not later than the first day of the seventh calendar month beginning after the month in which the President approves the report of the board which considered him for the second time." If an O-4 goes before the O-5 promotion board at the sixteenth (first consideration) and seventeenth (second consideration) year of service, involuntary separation might occur in the months immediately prior to the eighteenth year of service.

The eighteenth year of service is significant, as 10 U.S.C. 632 also stipulates that for an officer who would be separated on a date within two years of a normal retirement, the officer will "be retained on active duty until he is qualified for retirement and then retired under that section, unless he is sooner retired or discharged under another provision of law." If a normal career timeline includes consideration for O-5 at the sixteen-year point, opting out of consideration for promotion to either O-4 or O-5 precludes the possibility of involuntary separation.

As noted in the statute, officers must be in two broad categories to qualify for opt-out consideration. They must either be serving in a broadening assignment or be delayed in the completion of a career progression requirement because of a broadening assignment. In Appendix A (Robbert et al., 2021), we used cost-benefit analysis to help understand the circumstances under which opt out becomes an attractive option. Only some officers, and only those facing unique situations, might find opt out as an attractive policy from a financial perspective. Those circumstances include

- officers who expect a low probability of promotion under a normal timeline but an increased probability of promotion under opt out
- officers who qualify for a desirable broadening assignment only through a delay to the promotion timeline.

In other cases, as noted in Appendix A (Robbert et al., 2021), opt out might not substantially decrease expected financial compensation by delaying possible promotion for a year. In such cases, officers might find opt out to be an attractive option because the financial costs are relatively minor.

The pay system rewards increases in rank more than increases in tenure, leaving an officer who increases tenure without rank worse off than an officer who increases both longevity and rank at the same time. When the gain in rank occurs a year later, the perceived value of the pay increase will be smaller because a dollar today is worth more than a dollar next year. Opting out delays promotion in the near term and in many circumstances does not "pay for itself" with improved promotion prospects in the future. Even substantial gains in long-term promotion prospects, because those gains are often many years in the future, do not overcome the short-term loss that comes with delayed promotion.

Issue: Could the Department of Defense Advocate a Return to Permanent and Temporary Promotions?

This issue was framed in part as a means to increase the permeability of movement between active and reserve components but also as an approach to regain force management flexibilities that were afforded by having some officers initially appointed as *reserves serving on active duty* in what amounted to an extended probationary status. It invokes a pre-DOPMA framework in which most officers were initially commissioned as *reserve* officers serving on active duty and competed with regular officers for temporary promotions to higher grades. Some officers, such as military academy graduates, were commissioned as *regular* officers while those initially appointed as reserve officers on active duty were selectively *augmented* into the regular force at various career points. In addition to competing against each other for temporary promotions, regular officers and reserve officers serving on active duty also competed for permanent promotions in their separate regular and reserve promotion systems.

In the view of our project sponsor, the attractiveness of this pre-DOPMA framework was not the distinction between permanent and temporary promotions per se, but rather the distinction between regular and reserve commissions for officers on active duty. If reserve appointments for active-duty officers could be considered equivalent to appointments of officers in the reserve components (RCs), these officers could move between components without the need for reappointment scrolling.[5] Our evaluation in this section, summarized in Table 3.4, is thus focused in part on using reserve commissions for active-duty officers as an aid to active/reserve component permeability.

Our sponsor was also interested in the greater force management flexibilities that might be realized if some officers serving on active duty held reserve commissions. Chief among these is flexibility in managing tenure. As discussed in Appendix B (Robbert et al., 2021), reserve officers on active duty served "at the pleasure of the President" (10 U.S.C. 1162, 1976). Reserve officers serving on active duty provided flexibility to exceed the caps on regular officers in effect

---

[5] *Scrolling* is the term used for the processing of original appointment or certain promotions of officers. Some appointments are made by the Secretary of Defense under authorities delegated by the President. Other appointments are made by the President with the advice and consent of the Senate. A *scroll* refers to a list of officers forwarded to the appointing authority for such an appointment. Numerous potential sources of error and delay make scrolling an administratively challenging process. The transition from active to RCs currently requires a reappointment through this process due to a distinction in Title 10 between regular and reserve appointments. The services have sought legislative relief from this distinction, which has been found by the services to sometimes delay movement between components and to reduce reserve affiliations by officers separating from active duty. Section 501 of the FY 2020 NDAA requires a report on the feasibility of removing this distinction, thereby permitting movement between components without reappointment.

prior to DOPMA but also, due to their at-will tenure, provided a powerful mechanism for force reductions if needed.

Given this understanding of the issue, we have reframed it to focus on reserve commissions for officers on extended active duty. Table 3.4 reflects that reframing in its title. Our analysis considers whether pre-DOPMA practices that used this construct could be reimplemented under current statutory provisions.

Table 3.4. Reserve Commissions for Officers Serving on Extended Active Duty[a]

	Constraints?			
Domain	**Yes**	**No**	**Comments**	**Mitigation Strategy**
Statutory	X		In appointment provisions and accompanying definitions in 10 U.S.C., regular and reserve appointments are distinguished by the component in which they are made. There are no call-to-active-duty provisions suitable for placing reserve officers on extended active duty.	Propose legislation to provide reserve extended active duty provisions.
Policy	X		Many clarifying provisions likely required.	
Cultural	X		If reserve officers on active duty are seen as second-class citizens, morale and retention issues could arise.	
Fiscal		X		

[a] The original issue, a return to temporary and permanent promotions, is reframed here in terms of the sponsor's interest in the use of reserve commissions for active duty officers as an aid to active/reserve component permeability.

Background

Fully appreciating the motivation for this issue requires some background on both historic and contemporary usages of the terms *temporary* and *permanent* with respect to either grade ceilings or promotions. Appendix A provides a discussion of those usages (Robbert et al., 2021).

Constraints

Statutory

According to statutory provisions for appointment of officers and accompanying definitions, reserve officers serving on extended active duty would have to be appointed in an RC and then called to active duty. By the definitions provided in 10 U.S.C. 101, the term *regular,* with respect to appointment or grade, pertains to such office in a regular component of an armed force (10 U.S.C. 101(b)(12)). Similarly, the term *reserve* pertains to appointment or grade held as a *reserve* of one of the armed forces (10 U.S.C. 101(c)(6)). *Reserve*, with a capital *R*, is defined as consisting of three categories: Ready Reserve, Standby Reserve, and Retired Reserve (10 U.S.C.

10141(a)). To qualify as a reserve commission in the current statutory framework, an officer would have to be appointed in one of these three categories.

One approach would be to commission officers in the Individual Ready Reserve and then voluntarily call them to active duty. Currently, 10 U.S.C. 12301(d) contains the only provision for a voluntary call to active duty and is the only call-to-active-duty provision that might approach suitability for this purpose. As indicated in Table 3.5, all other call-to-active-duty provisions are involuntary, time-limited, restricted to time of war or national emergency, and/or restricted to units rather than individuals.

Table 3.5. Statutory Provisions for Involuntary Call to Active Duty

10 U.S.C. Section	Purpose	Unit	Individual	Time Limit
12301(a)	War/national emergency declared by Congress or authorized by law	X	X	War/emergency plus 6 months
12301(b)	Not specified	X	X	15 days per year
12302	National emergency declared by President	X	X	24 months
12303	Unsatisfactory participation		X	24 months
12304	Named operational mission	X	X	365 days
12304a	Federal assistance requested by governor	X	X	120 days
12304b	Preplanned missions in support of combatant command	X		365 days

Using Section 12301(d) authority to place reserve officers on extended active duty entails some strength accountability issues. It is included in a category of reservists on active duty for operational support whose overall numbers must be annually authorized by law (10 U.S.C. 115(b)(1)(A)). For example, the FY 2020 NDAA specifies that 13,000 Army reservists (all personnel, not just officers) may be on active duty under 10 U.S.C. 115(b) in FY 2020. This provision is apparently intended to limit the degree to which the RCs can be used to augment authorized active-duty strengths. Enlarging this number to accommodate a significant proportion of the active officer force would appear to defeat Congress's interest in limiting the number of reservists augmenting active-duty strength. Note, however, that if called for a period of service exceeding three years or cumulative periods exceeding 1,095 out of 1,460 days, these reserve officers on extended active duty would also be counted in active-duty end strength (10 U.S.C. 115(b)(2)). More problematically, officers called up under 10 U.S.C. 12301(d) would not be counted in the field-grade ceilings prescribed in 10 U.S.C. 523(a).[6] This would seem to be inconsistent with the DOPMA objective of managing all officers on extended active duty under a single grade and promotion structure.

Another complication in using 10 U.S.C. 12301(d) for extended active duty is that these officers are excluded from the *active-duty lists* used to manage officers for active-duty promotions (10 U.S.C. 641(1)(A)) and therefore would not compete against regular officers for promotions.[7] Instead, they would be carried on the reserve active-status list of their military force and would compete for promotion with reserve officers not on active duty. This too would be inconsistent with a single active-duty grade and promotion structure. The provisions for temporary promotions or a temporary grade structure, used in the pre-DOPMA framework to provide a way for regular officers and reserve officers on extended active duty to compete against each other in promotion considerations, no longer exist.

Another set of issues to be considered is tenure of reserve officers on extended active duty if called up using 10 U.S.C. 12301(d). Their tenure would not be managed by conventional up-or-out or force-shaping authorities for officers on active duty, all of which are contained in a chapter of Title 10 that applies to officers on the active-duty list, which excludes officers called up under 10 U.S.C. 12301(d). Instead, the provisions of 10 U.S.C. 12313 would apply; subject to certain restrictions, the secretary concerned may at any time release a Reserve from active duty. One such restriction is the provision for active-duty agreements under 10 U.S.C. 12311. These provide for renewable terms of up to five years, require board approval for early release without consent due to force reduction, allow for early release if twice deferred for promotion, and allow for involuntary retention during a war or national emergency. Without an active-duty agreement, a Reserve serves on active duty at the will of a service secretary.

To make 12301(d) call-up palatable as a vehicle for placing reserve officers on extended active duty, a legislative change would be required to exclude them from the categories of reservists covered by 10 U.S.C. 115(b)(1), thereby subjecting them to the same strength, grade-ceiling, and promotion-management list provisions as regular officers. However, doing so would eliminate the provisions that make 12301(d) a suitable vehicle for voluntary call-up of part-time reservists to provide shorter-term, temporary operational support. A more straightforward approach would be to legislate a new call-up authority specifically for reserve officers serving on extended active duty, with specified strength-accounting, grade-ceiling, promotion, and tenure provisions. If new legislation is proposed to accommodate reserve officers serving on extended

---

[6] In determining authorized grade strengths, 10 U.S.C. 523(b)(1)(A) excludes reserve officers on active duty under 10 U.S.C. 115(b)(1); that is, reservists on active duty whose numbers must be separately authorized by law. 10 U.S.C. 115(b)(1), in turn, includes officers on active duty under 10 U.S.C. 12301(d).

[7] 10 U.S.C. 620 specifies that officers on active duty will be carried on the active-duty list of their armed force, but 10 U.S.C. 641(1)(A) provides an exception for officers on active duty under 10 U.S.C. 115(b)(1). 10 U.S.C. 115(b)(1), in turn, includes officers on active duty under 10 U.S.C. 12301(d).

active duty, it could be fashioned to provide additional personnel management flexibilities not currently available for military personnel. For example, it might provide an option for reserve officers on extended active duty to work part-time rather than full-time schedules.

Legislative changes to eliminate separate active and reserve scrolling requirements would not eliminate the issues discussed in the preceding paragraphs. 10 U.S.C. 12301 and other call-up provisions pertain equally to commissioned officers, WOs, and enlisted personnel, while only commissioned officers are affected by scrolling requirements. With undifferentiated officer appointment scrolls, reserve officers called to active duty would be managed in the same way as reserve enlisted personnel called to active duty. They would remain members of a Reserve, as defined in 10 U.S.C. 10141, whether or not on active duty, until such time as a service secretary accepted them for transfer to an active component (AC).

Policy

A completely new set of DoD and service policies and procedures would have to be established to enable this change. The policies could borrow from historic precedents, but would have to address a range of personnel issues, including appointments, promotions, and augmentation from reserve to regular status.

Cultural

Cultural tensions are a perennial issue in discussions of permeability between the active and reserve components. For more on this, see our discussion of active/reserve permeability in Chapter 5.

Service Perspectives

All services have advocated streamlined procedures for transitions between active and reserve components. No service expressed an interest in a return to reserve commissions for active-duty officers, but all favor elimination of the requirement for rescrolling when changing components.

Proposed Way Forward

As a step toward permeability, restoration of provisions for reserve officers to serve on extended active duty seems intended as a second option if movement toward a single scrolling procedure is foreclosed. However, the statutory and policy changes required for this arrangement seem to be as least as sweeping as those required for single scrolling. Moreover, the impact on permeability would be much less than that of single scrolling. Accordingly, we see single scrolling as a clearly preferred option.

As a vehicle for enhanced flexibility in officer force management, currently available call-up authorities are problematic for the purpose of maintaining a large contingent of reserve officers on extended active duty. New authorities, similar to those for reserve officers on extended active duty found in pre-DOPMA versions of Title 10 and tailored to the purposes at hand, would be required.

Issue: Could the Department of Defense Recommend Selection Board Guidance Regarding Deployability?

Introducing deployability to selection board guidance brings together several key concepts that must be defined and explored. We do so in a sequential manner. First, we consider the statutory requirements for board guidance and the current policy implementation of the requirement, as well as limitations on who might be deployed according to statute. Next, we describe the current approach to evaluating and measuring deployability and highlight several considerations when evaluating nondeployability. To assist in answering whether the department should recommend selection board guidance, we highlight recent RAND research into the implications of deployability and operational fitness for a military career. Finally, we will recommend several considerations for the department if it were to consider linking promotion selection to deployability. Key considerations are summarized in Table 3.6.

Table 3.6. Promotion Board Guidance for Deployability

	Constraints?			
Domain	**Yes**	**No**	**Comments**	**Mitigation Strategy**
Statutory		X	615 provides wide latitude for promotion board guidance. Statute is largely silent on deployability definition. 615 mandates that only "substantiated, relevant information" be included in information that goes to the board.	Deployability information could go before a promotion board if included in officer performance evaluations. Nonstatutory boards also offer an example, such as Army command boards that require a memorandum certifying deployability.
Policy	X		Definitions of deployability are established via policy and can change over time or by theater. Dwell-time policies historically are the largest driver of nondeployability.	
Cultural	X		Nondeployability already adversely affects career, and can be heavily influenced by luck and timing (especially temporary nondeployability). Stronger consequences for temporary conditions would violate sense of fairness and egalitarianism.	Ramifications for permanent nondeployability might meet less cultural resistance than ramifications for temporary nondeployability.
Fiscal		X	Could have negative retention impacts, but fiscal impact might be favorable if reduced force costs are less than increased training costs.	

Constraints

Statutory

As indicated in Table 3.6, current law appears to allow for the inclusion of references to deployability in board guidance. 10 U.S.C. 615 requires that the secretary of a military department furnish to a selection board "information or guidelines relating to the needs of the armed force concerned for officers having particular skills." DoD Instruction 1320.14 implements the law, requiring that the secretaries of the military departments "furnish information and written instructions to promotion selection boards," including "information or guidelines on the needs of the Service concerned for officers having particular skills" (2019, p. 14). Neither law nor policy constrains the definition of particular skills, which in turn might allow the inclusion of deployability as a desired "skill" for consideration. DoDI 1320.14 prohibits all DoD officials from "direct[ing] that a particular individual be selected or not be selected by a promotion or special selection board" (2019, p. 8). There are few examples of explicit career benchmarks that an officer must meet to be selected for promotion.[8]

Law and its implementing policy define the type of information about individual officers that may be brought before a selection board but set broad limits on such information. "Information that is in the officer's official military personnel file" comprises the bulk of such information, along with communication from the officer to the board and a narrow category of "substantiated, relevant information that could reasonably and materially affect the deliberations of the selection board" (10 U.S.C. 615).

Explicit information regarding deployability could reasonably be included in an official military personnel file in the future, though the military services do not routinely include direct references to deployability. Many services tangentially address deployability. For instance, services may require comments on performance evaluations regarding physical fitness; the inability to meet current physical fitness standards because of injury or illness could be an imperfect proxy for deployability.

The Army explicitly addressed deployability in the FY 2020 selection board for O-5 and O-6 command and key billet opportunities, known as a *centralized selection list* (CSL) board. Officers electing to compete in the board had to submit a memorandum "that that they have no permanent medical or physical restriction on world-wide deployability" (Department of the Army, 2018). The memorandum in turn became part of the information provided to the CSL board. The Army CSL board differs from a promotion board in a fundamental way, however: A CSL board is an "opt-in" board in which officers elect to compete, while a promotion board considers all officers in the competitive category and the promotion zone. Additionally, a CSL board is a nonstatutory board and operates outside of the constraints of Title 10.

[8] For instance, one such benchmark is the requirement for an officer to be designated as a joint qualified officer prior to an appointment as an O-7 (10 U.S.C. 619a).

Title 10 provides few limitations on the military services regarding deployability. 10 U.S.C. 671 stipulates that a service member "may not be assigned to active duty on land outside the United States" prior to the completion of basic military training requirements, which in a time of war or national emergency may not be less than twelve weeks. 18 U.S.C. 922, popularly known as the Lautenberg Amendment, prohibits carrying firearms if convicted of misdemeanor domestic violence. Other deployability considerations emerge through policy, rather than through statute.

Policy

Deployability policy changes over time for many reasons. The requirements of deployment locations change, and if one deployment location offers services unavailable in another deployment location, some service members could be considered nondeployable for the latter location. Responses to the underlying nondeployability reason might also shift, as concerns over some conditions lead to new categorization while improved treatment removes nondeployability from others.

Current DoD policy, as reflected in DoDI 1332.45 (2018), creates categories for nondeployability, dividing nondeployability into permanent and temporary categories and additional subcategories of medical, administrative, and legal. The policy explicitly states that "all Service members are expected to be deployable" (p. 4).

Service members might experience a period of nondeployability for many different reasons. Drawing from DoDI 1332.45, Table 3.7 provides a summary of the current categorization for temporary and permanent nondeployability. Other reasons, not reflected in the table, include a current deployment, initial training participation, service academy attendance, long educational course attendance, or being on the move between duty stations (collectively referred to as *transients and training*). In addition, service members who require a periodic health assessment, dental work, or a hearing test are nondeployable, but those situations can be rectified quickly.

Table 3.7. Temporary and Permanent Nondeployable Categories

Category	Temporary	Permanent
Medical	Patient Medical condition that limits full duty Pregnancy (including postpartum)	Permanent limited duty Enrolled in disability evaluation system Permanent profile nonduty related action (RC only)
Administrative	Absent without leave Family care plan Adoption Service member under 18 Humanitarian assignment Service discretion Pending administrative separation Unsatisfactory participants or administrative action pending (RC only)	Sole survivor, surviving family member, or deferred from hostile fire zone Unable to carry firearm Conscientious objector
Legal	Prisoner Legal action	

SOURCE: DoDI 1332.45, 2018, pp. 9–11.

Some temporary nondeployable conditions might correspond to circumstances that will terminate military service. A service member who is absent without leave might be dropped from the rolls. A service member pending administrative separation is, by definition, soon to exit the military. A service member facing legal action might, if convicted, face involuntary separation, as might a prisoner. Nondeployability is a side effect of circumstances that will often lead to near-term separation from the service.

In other cases, temporary nondeployability can lead to permanent nondeployability. A service member who has been nondeployable for twelve months or longer due to a medical condition must be referred to the Disability Evaluation System (DoDI 1332.18, 2018, p. 26), which changes the nondeployability to a permanent status.[9] Those found unfit for duty through the Disability Evaluation System will be separated from military service, unless approved for retention with a waiver.

Cultural

Currently, no military service directly reflects deployability status in performance evaluations. Deployability is not a box to check or a comment to address in performance evaluations. We see logic in its explicit exclusion from performance evaluations. While some nondeployable conditions in the legal or administrative categories represent failures to accomplish military requirements or adhere to military discipline, other nondeployable conditions might strike unpredictably, represent desirable personal and family outcomes, or result from injuries sustained due to military service.

Performance evaluations may indirectly address nondeployability for certain conditions. If a service member is nondeployable for a temporary medical condition, the service member might be unable to perform a required physical fitness test on a normal schedule. Physical fitness test results are often included in performance evaluations.

Many nondeployable categories represent conditions that will affect a service member's job performance over the short term in addition to preventing the service member from deploying. Lack of a family care plan, for instance, might constrain work performance because the service member cannot accommodate temporary duty (TDY) or unusual duty hours. Legal action, such as being under investigation, might limit access to government information.

A medical condition that limits full duty deserves particular exploration, as medical conditions can strike unpredictably. We define a *medical condition* as one that limits full duty for a period of thirty days or more but less than twelve months, as opposed to a condition that is far more acute. An illness or injury that degrades duty performance for two weeks might be

---

[9] Pregnant and postpartum service members are exempt from referral to the Disability Evaluation System (DoDI 1332.45, 2018, p. 16).

significant for the individual and unit in the near term, but that isolated incident will likely not substantially influence a performance evaluation. Illness and injury can strike at random, and anyone can get significantly sick occasionally.

However, some people may be unlucky; their temporary medical condition can exceed 30 days and stretch into several months. In such cases, a service member's temporary medical condition could influence both performance evaluations and career trajectories. Consider a hypothetical situation. A service member is slated to deploy with a unit in approximately 60 days, but severely breaks his leg and requires six months to recover. The service member will be unable to perform his duties on the deployment and instead will stay at home station. A different service member will assume the deployed duties. The service member's scope of responsibility might have been greater during the deployment than at home station. By the time the service member fully recovers, he will have missed much or all of the deployment and a change in duties, both of which represent potentially falling behind peers. The opportunity cost of a broken leg might be high.

Such an unlucky event will eventually leach into selection board outcomes. Drawing from the hypothetical case above, we can see that our unlucky service member's performance record will look different from his peers: He is missing a deployment and has a different collection of jobs held. Even after he makes a full recovery, he is left with suboptimal experiences compared with his never-injured peers.

Fortunately, such an outcome should be rare. Most illnesses and injuries are short, and even those that exceed 30 days are often unlikely to have grave operational or career effects. However, some temporary conditions, including adoption and pregnancy, are not randomly assigned, can be welcomed by those who experience it, and might impact performance evaluations.

Recent RAND research (Hall et al., 2019) explored concerns about pregnancy and performance evaluations in a project that identified barriers to female retention in the United States Coast Guard. Although the Coast Guard is part of the Department of Homeland Security, many of the dynamics influencing female members of the Coast Guard resemble circumstances in military departments in DoD. The research team developed the following insight during their focus groups:

> Some participants expressed frustration regarding how pregnancy affects evaluations. Pregnancies are not indicated on evaluations; however, members must keep to the same evaluation schedule and time line. As a result, they will show fewer accomplishments than their peers because of their time away on parental leave or having had limited duty while pregnant. Women noted that this resulted in less competitive evaluations during these periods, without explanation. (Hall et al., 2019, p. 40)

An extended period in which a service member is unable to perform full duties, such as pregnancy and being postpartum, might negatively impact performance evaluations. Extended periods of injury and illness are less well-studied than pregnancy, but it is reasonable to infer that the same dynamics will be at work—namely, those unable to perform the full duties for an extended period will receive less competitive evaluations.

Service Perspectives

In our discussions with service representatives, we heard no interest from any service for adding explicit deployability information to an officer's performance record. As Navy representatives stated, career advancement requires deployability and thus creates an incentive to remain deployable.[10]

Proposed Way Forward

Moving forward, it may be appropriate to maintain the status quo. From discussions with the services, the current focus on deployability using existing tools and policies allows the services to adequately manage nondeployability.

If the services do decide to pursue deployability in board guidance, they may wish to consider differentiating between types of nondeployability, such as focusing on permanent medical nondeployability or those enrolled in the Integrated Disability Evaluation System (IDES).[11] Temporary nondeployability, by its very definition, will be resolved in one of three ways: by resolution of the situation, by separation from the service, or by transfer to a permanent nondeployability status. Those promoted to a higher rank with a permanent deployability limitation will likely present a bigger burden to the service than those promoted with a temporary limitation, given that most temporary limitations are of short duration.

An alternative approach, which would require a statute change, could include IDES enrollment as a mandatory basis for a consideration to opt-out of promotion. Currently, all officers in the promotion zone within a given competitive category compete for promotion. With a statute change, officers could opt out, on either a mandatory or a voluntary basis, of promotion consideration if enrolled in IDES. By opting out, the service removes the possibility that an officer selected for promotion could imminently be separated from the service through IDES. At the same time, such a statute change would create the incentive for an officer to stall IDES enrollment until after promotion consideration.

Other Considerations

Selection boards already indirectly consider information on extended nondeployability. Selection boards review performance records, which incorporate the duties and performance of

[10] Discussion with U.S. Navy representatives, September 17, 2019.

[11] IDES helps the DoD determine if wounded, ill, or injured service members are able to continue to serve. DoD and the Department of Veterans Affairs have joined together to create IDES, which combines two formerly separate and sequential disability systems into one process.

the considered population. Officers facing extended periods of nondeployability perform different duties and functions than their fully deployable peers. This dynamic removes some of the impetus for selection board guidance. However, under the same dynamic, selection boards might inadvertently discriminate against female officers who have been pregnant compared with female officers who have not been pregnant.

It also should be noted that tying promotion outcomes to snapshots of deployability status may create incentives to delay needed medical evaluation until after promotion boards. In some circumstances, officers determine the timing of nondeployability. An officer can schedule a needed surgery one month or delay it several months, for example. If an officer requires medical attention, but that medical attention carries promotion risk, the officer might time such activities to limit the possibility of adverse promotion outcomes.

4. Tenure

This chapter discusses the three issues related to various aspects of officer tenure management:

- Could promotion boards have more liberal show-cause provisions to account for stagnant officers? What are the limits of the current provisions in this regard?
- Given the legislative change removing the requirement to achieve 20 years of commissioned service by age 62, what controls, if any, could be put in place?
- What statutory and policy changes are required for officers to be contracted the way that enlisted members are today and what are the pros and cons of doing so?

Issue: Could Promotion Boards Have More Liberal Show-Cause Provisions to Account for Stagnant Officers? What Are the Limits of the Current Provisions in This Regard?

In recent years, the Army and Navy used selective early retirement boards (SERBs) to involuntarily remove officers, especially in the grades of O-5 and O-6. As with any board in which performance records are considered, a SERB improves the overall distribution of quality by removing those below a certain quality cut-off. The circumstances in each of the services markedly differ. In the Army's case, the service faced declining end strength and instituted retirement boards to meet force structure goals. In the Navy's case, using enhanced selective early retirement board (eSERB) authority, the service reviewed the performance records of a broad swath of O-5s on an annual basis to meet desired quality levels. SERB or eSERB is just one of several mechanisms for removing officers from active duty, although each mechanism faces several constraints by law.

The research sponsor desired to know if the authorities of 10 U.S.C. 1181 could be more liberally applied to remove stagnant officers. Section 1181 established that, in specified circumstances, an officer must show cause for retention on active duty, a process commonly referred to as *show cause*. In discussions with the research sponsor, we agreed to review the various mechanisms for removing officers and offered alternatives for future consideration.

Any discussion of "stagnant" officers should begin with a definition of the word; *Merriam Webster's Dictionary* defines the term as "not advancing or developing." A stagnant officer is thus one who is no longer advancing or developing beyond the current grade. The dictionary definition does not match common usage, whereby *stagnant* has a negative connotation that is inappropriate in a hierarchical organization where most members—eventually—will no longer advance. In consultation with the research sponsor, we recommended a working definition of *stagnant* that entails a perception of low performance and long tenure. This is separate from an officer who fails to meet the standards of the grade or engages in misconduct.

At its essence, the primary purpose behind the up-or-out system is the removal of stagnant officers and their replacement by younger, more vigorous officers.[1] As Rostker (2015, p. 9) noted in congressional testimony, "Our officers need to progress or leave. They must not be allowed to stagnate in place." The logic of the tenure system relies on the propensity for decreased productivity later in a career. Those who are most productive may be promoted, but those with declining productivity—those who lack the "physical and mental endurance" (Goldich, 1995, p. 5) of younger officers—must be removed from the service. A retirement incentive, a vested pension at 20 years of service, encourages departures from military service without the use of separation boards.[2] Using the language of economists, Asch and Warner (2001, pp. 552–553) observed, "The only truly unique role of retired pay in existing models is to solve an 'end-of-period' incentive problem that arises when the opportunity cost of an older worker's time falls below on-the-job productivity but the individual will not retire because pay also exceeds opportunity cost (and productivity)."

Such an inducement leads to a large-scale departure from the military around the twentieth year of service and shortly thereafter. It does not, however, forcibly remove officers from the service. Retirement remains voluntary unless compelled through one of the mechanisms discussed below. Whether the 20-year retirement is sufficiently attractive to encourage the retirement of the least productive officers can be difficult to determine. With each subsequent year of service, an unproductive officer can slightly increase future pension payments. Highly unproductive officers may remain in the military longer, waiting until the cost of remaining in the service equals the benefits from staying in the service. For most officers who are neither advancing nor developing, the retirement inducement likely creates a sufficient incentive to leave the service. That same inducement might be even more effective for more productive officers, given that their options outside the military might be more plentiful, fulfilling, or remunerative.

Using DMDC data, we reviewed the career experiences of O-5s across the military departments from 2001–2018, focusing on the period when an officer without prior enlisted service would become eligible for military retirement. As indicated in Figures 4.1 and 4.2, the population declines sharply with each passing year, down about 50 percent by the twenty-second year of service. Each service loses at least 80 percent of its O-5s—either to retirement or promotion to O-6—by the twenty-fourth year of active commissioned service. The following year, only the Army retains over 10 percent of its initial population of O-5s at the grade of O-5.

---

[1] Older officers must depart to ensure promotion opportunities for younger officers. Both promotion opportunity (the maximum number who could get promoted divided by those considered) and promotion timing (the total months of service at the point of promotion) are influenced by the departure of those at a higher rank (DoD, 2019).

[2] The Blended Retirement System (BRS) introduces new considerations that, in future years, might change the importance of pension eligibility at the twentieth year of service. We address these considerations later in the report.

Figure 4.1. Average O-5 Population, 2008–2013, by Service and Years of Active Commissioned Service

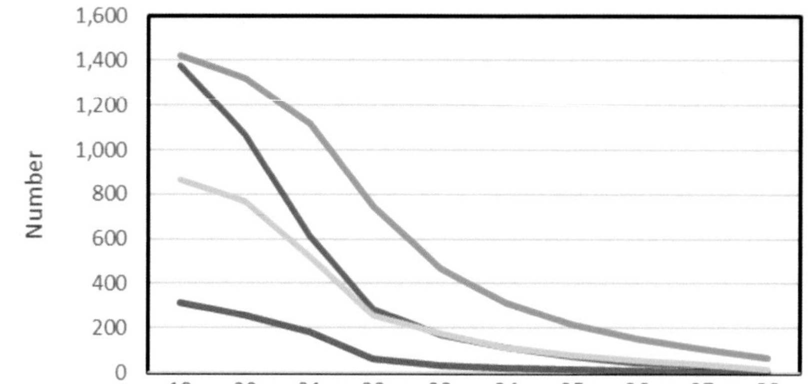

	19	20	21	22	23	24	25	26	27	28
Air Force	1,378	1,069	610	284	169	114	72	46	32	4
Army	1,424	1,318	1,118	743	470	315	219	152	109	66
Marine Corps	314	259	180	58	34	18	13	9	6	3
Navy	868	767	520	257	174	114	81	55	41	14

NOTE: We selected the period 2008–2013 to best estimate O-5 retention in a policy-free environment. Prior to 2008, large-scale overseas deployments might have influenced retention behavior, and after 2013 some services entered a period of declining end strength and accompanying early retirement boards.

Figure 4.2. Percentage of O-5 Population, 2008–2013, Remaining After 19 Years of Service, by Service and Years of Active Commissioned Service

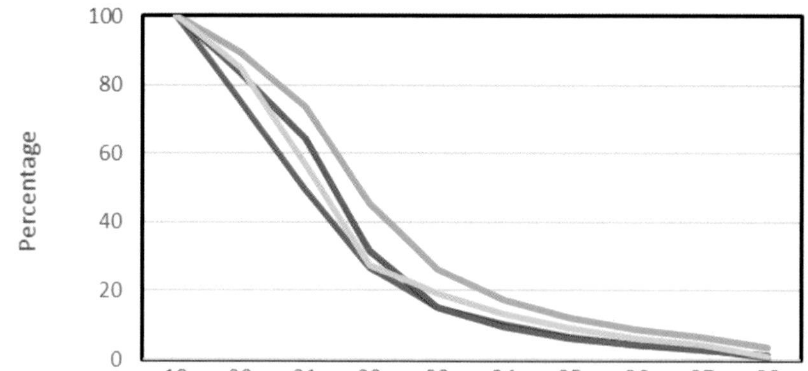

	19	20	21	22	23	24	25	26	27	28
Air Force	100	75	50	27	15	10	7	4	3	0
Army	100	89	74	45	26	17	12	9	6	4
Marine Corps	100	83	64	31	15	10	6	4	3	1
Navy	100	85	57	28	19	13	9	6	4	1

These data show that a limited number of long-tenured officers with low promotion prospects remain in service. However, the numbers may be great enough to warrant OSD and service attention. Accordingly, Table 4.1 addresses applicable constraints and mitigation strategies.

Table 4.1. More Liberal Provisions for Stagnant Officers

Domain	Constraints? Yes	Constraints? No	Comments	Mitigation Strategy
Statutory	X		Several options for removing stagnant officers exist, but none is well-suited for below-average performers of long tenure.	A nonstatutory and costly mechanism for enticing stagnant officers to depart is through undesirable assignments.
			For O-5s, 20-year retirement cliff encourages departure, but they could remain to 28 years.	A statute change could compel involuntary retirement for twice failure of selection to O-6.
			Statute applies to all officers across all competitive categories.	A statute change could allow contracts for service beyond 20 years.
Policy	X		Circumstances for SERB/eSERB use (force-shaping versus culling).	Greater clarity on whether SERB/eSERB meant for force-shaping or strictly for performance culling.
				New promotion authorities (temporary promotion and alternate promotion authority) might reduce likelihood of promotion for less productive officers.
				Increased attention to job matches might encourage productive officers to remain and provide more appropriate matches across productivity spectrum.
Cultural	X		Organization places more emphasis on those with promotion potential than those without.	
			Differentiating quality within grade is a challenge.	
Fiscal		X	Could have negative retention impacts, but fiscal impact might be favorable if reduced force costs are less than increased training costs.	

Constraints

Current law provides one primary mechanism for removing stagnant officers from the service: tenure management provisions of the up-or-out system. But that system introduces legal, policy, and cultural constraints that require the services to rely on relatively blunt instruments (selective early retirement, show cause for retention, and force shaping) that may not be well tailored to specifically removing stagnant officers as defined here.

Statutory

The up-or-out system uses rank-dependent measures to remove stagnant officers during a military career.[3] Officers in the grade of O-3 and O-4 will be removed through involuntary

[3] 10 U.S.C. 532 caps the number of commissioned officers in the grades of O-4 to O-6 for each service, with exceptions for situations such as reserve officers on active duty in some circumstances, medical officers, dental officers, and general or flag officers.

separation after having twice failed of selection for promotion (10 U.S.C. 632).[4] The law requires the removal of the affected officer by the first day of the seventh month after the approval of the board results. Officers who are retirement-eligible or will be retirement-eligible within two years will be retired. Importantly, officers in the grades of O-5 and above are not subject to the same provisions.

The up-or-out system removes stagnant O-5s and O-6s through separate tenure management provisions. Unlike more junior officers, these officers are not subject to involuntary separation after twice failing of selection for promotion. Rather, the law caps the maximum active commissioned service. For O-5s, 10 U.S.C. 633 limits service to 28 years. For O-6s, 10 U.S.C. 634 limits service to 30 years.

Officers in the grades of O-5 through O-8 may be removed from active duty through selective early retirement under 10 U.S.C. 638. Using a selection board, a specified number of officers will be selected for early retirement, not to exceed more than 30 percent of those eligible. Officers selected for early retirement will retire at the date of their choosing or not later than the first day of the seventh month after the approval of the board results. The law provides eligibility limitations for selective early retirement for O-5s through O-8s. Specifically with regard to O-5s and O-6s,

- O-5s must have twice failed of selection for promotion to O-6 and not be on a list of officers recommended for promotion to O-6
- O-6s must have served at least four years on active duty in that grade and not on a list of officers recommended for promotion to O-7.

10 U.S.C. 638 provides that officers may be considered by a board for selective early retirement only once in that grade within a five-year period. 10 U.S.C. 638a provides enhanced authority to waive the five-year provision if the Secretary of Defense determines that the Secretary of a military department needs such authority.

10 U.S.C. 638a provides other enhanced authorities for separation boards. The Secretary of Defense may authorize the secretary of a military department to use those authorities, which include

- early retirement of O-5s from any service if they failed of selection for promotion at least one time and are not on a list of officers recommended for promotion to O-6
- early retirement of O-6s from any service who have served on active duty in that grade for at least two years and are not on a list of officers recommended for promotion to O-7.

---

[4] 10 U.S.C. 637 provides a mechanism for the military service to selectively continue a military officer who would otherwise be separated from the service. The military services frequently use this authority, though its use varies over time. For instance, the Army selectively continued 87–94 percent of O-4s across its four line competitive categories who were twice failed of selection in FY 2018, but selectively continued less than 10 percent of the same population in 2013 (Department of the Army, Office of the Deputy Chief of Staff G-1, 2013, 2018).

The Army used authorities in 638 and 638a to significantly reduce the population of O-5s and O-6s in 2013–2014, selecting for early retirement over 500 officers in those grades to meet end strength goals in the Army.[5] This use of separation authorities—used in a time of restructuring the force—contrasts with the Navy's approach to the separation authorities described under the Services Perspective heading below.

In addition to the separation boards described above, a military service can also use force-shaping authority as described in 10 U.S.C. 647. The authority allows the secretary of a military department to discharge or transfer an officer solely for the purpose of restructuring an armed force. Because the authority resides with a service secretary rather than the Secretary of Defense, OSD does not publish guidance on the authority's use. Two categories of officers can be affected by the authority:

- officers with less than six years of service as a commissioned officer
- officers with more than six years of service as a commissioned "but ha[ve] not completed a minimum service obligation applicable to that member."

The limitations on service generally prevent the use of this authority on officers above the grade of O-3, as they would have accrued more than six years of service at that point in a career.[6] Beyond that limitation, the force-shaping authority affords broad latitude to the service. It is not limited by considerations of competitive category or a maximum number of officers that can be discharged.

The Marine Corps makes regular use of force shaping authority in its Career Designation Program. The Career Designation Program considers officers around the fifth year of service for retention on the active-duty list. "Career designation is the competitive process used to determine which company grade officers will be offered the opportunity for continued active service beyond their initial active service obligation" (U.S. Marine Corps, 2014, p. 5). Officers selected through an officer retention board achieve career designation status; those not selected separate from active duty at the end of their service obligation.

Finally, the law provides a mechanism for removing an officer if the officer fails to show cause for retention on active duty. 10 U.S.C. 1181 requires that the military departments establish procedures to review the record of any commissioned officer to determine whether the officer be required to show cause for retention on active duty. Two scenarios arise that justify such a situation:

- "because his performance of duty has fallen below standards prescribed by the Secretary of Defense"

---

[5] Information provided by Officer Force Management Policy via email.

[6] Commissioned officers are in a probationary status until the completion of six years of active commissioned service (10 U.S.C. 630).

- "because of misconduct, because of moral or professional dereliction, or because his retention is not clearly consistent with the interests of national security."

Whereas involuntary separation through twice failure of selection for promotion or through early retirement involves a selection board convened through 10 U.S.C. 611, the show-cause process uses a board of inquiry as described in 10 U.S.C. 1182. The board of inquiry process limits consideration to individual cases, rather than the more large-scale results that can be achieved through other selection board–driven mechanisms. 10 U.S.C. 1186 allows the military department secretary, at any time during the proceedings, to grant a request by the considered officer to voluntarily retire if qualified or to be discharged. An officer removed from active duty through show-cause proceedings will be retired if qualified.

As constructed in law, show cause as a process contains two facets that suppress its use. A board of inquiry is administratively onerous at the command level, especially compared with a separation board. A separation board might be likewise costly to execute, but those costs are dispersed across the entire service. In addition, a board of inquiry might result in the near-immediate separation of an officer from the service, which is a result of such magnitude that it effectively limits show-cause proceedings to rare cases. By comparison, an officer designated for separation through a board will be separated several months later.

Policy

SERB and eSERB authorities provide the military services with options for removing stagnant officers, but it is not clear which circumstances call for their use. Is the goal of removing stagnant officers sufficient to warrant SERB or eSERB, or is force restructuring also required? All separation boards involve differentiation by officer quality, but it is not clear if SERB or eSERB can be used exclusively to remove stagnant officers. Greater policy clarity would help the situation.

Cultural

Among officers who are not likely to be promoted again, differentiating between productive and unproductive officers can be a challenge. The promotion system struggles to "recognize significant within-rank differences" (Warner, 2008, p. 12), and military performance evaluation systems are designed around promotion decisions rather than decisions about in-rank retention. Some services use separate procedures for rectifying this situation, most often in response to separation boards. The Air Force, for instance, uses a retention recommendation form to require senior officers provide "performance-based differentiation and retention recommendations" on their subordinates (Department of the Air Force, 2016, p. 266).

Because of the challenge of recognizing in-rank differences, a dichotomous situation may emerge: at any given rank, one might be likely to be promoted or unlikely to be promoted. As a hierarchical organization, the military values promotion potential. Many organizations tend to ignore "effectively performing managers with low likelihoods of promotion" (Carnazza et al.,

1981, p. 22). Officers with high promotion potential and their low-performing peers will receive relatively more interest from the service, to the exclusion of capable performers. This greater interest can manifest itself through more attention to job assignments. In the case of low-performing officers, an informal mechanism for encouraging voluntary retirement is through less desirable posting. This is a potentially costly mechanism, as it associates certain assignments with low-performing officers and might dissuade more effective officers from such postings. For those "effectively performing managers," however, less interest and attention to job assignment decisions might result in alignments that yield lower levels of performance, whether through a mismatch of skills or lower job satisfaction. As a result, the services might perceive that a swath of officers provide middling performance without recognizing that a dearth of service-level attention led to the predicament.

In some circumstances, military departments might detect a level of performance among officers of long tenure that significantly departs from the actual level of capability of that population. In Appendix D (Robbert et al., 2021), we created a model of a military career and simulated the effect of imprecision in performance assessments, job assignments, and job performance when poorly matched to the job. Our results suggest that for officers who fail of selection to O-6, significant disparities might emerge between what the services observe in performance and what these same officers could deliver.

Service Perspectives

Service representatives highlighted the challenge of addressing low-performing officers of long tenure. Navy representatives discussed how their service employs eSERB authorities to cull stagnant officers, removing approximately 33 officers annually in the grades of O-5 and O-6. Most officers, however, were not stagnant in the sense that they were low performing with long tenure. Instead, according to Navy representatives, most had significant blemishes on their performance record. The Navy intends to pursue eSERB on an annual basis, as a type of performance file review. We asked the Navy why it used eSERB rather than show-cause proceedings. The Navy representatives expressed that an eSERB allows a corporate review of performance records on a large scale, as opposed to a narrow and focused board of inquiry.

Army representatives recommended the use of the term "low-demand talent" to describe stagnant officers. Current and upcoming efforts by the Army to better align officers to units through mutually agreed talent matching might signal to some officers that their talents are no longer in demand and raise performance because officers will be motivated by the opportunity to choose from a set of available new challenges.

Marine Corps representatives discussed the dual challenge of long tenured officers. *Commandant's Planning Guidance* (Department of the Navy, 2019b) provides instructions that require nuance in application. On the one hand, "We must seek the administrative separation of those unable to be promoted who are creating an artificial barrier for advancement of more motivated individuals" (p. 7). On the other, there is an emphasis on reforming policies that "throw away talent at the point it is most productive and highly trained, and discourage performers who would like to continue serving, but may be less interested in promotion or constant disruptive moves of questionable personal and professional value" (p. 7).

Air Force representatives discussed a variety of hypothetical measures for removing low-performing officers of long tenure, all of which would require potential statute changes. The overarching theme was a desire to more promptly and systematically remove officers who are no longer highly motivated. Ideas included removing officers through a more liberal and yet less draconian show-cause process, an annual board designed around retention decisions, or a contract system for O-6s.

Proposed Way Forward

The military departments have many tools that allow them to incentivize, and if necessary compel, retirement for AC officers. None of the current tools is especially well-suited for removing stagnant officers from the service in a timely manner, especially if those same officers balk at retiring around 20 years. Current law suspends separation for officers who twice fail of selection to O-6 or O-7. SERBs presuppose a need to cull a competitive category for force-shaping reasons, rather than for purely quality-control reasons. The show-cause provisions are administratively onerous, and substandard performance might be difficult to document and quantify. Equally important to the statutory constraints are limits of foresight and knowledge. The military services will promote some individuals who might not deserve to be promoted, misidentifying temporary and fluctuating performance for underlying long-term potential. Similarly, the military services might struggle to distinguish productive officers from unproductive officers within the category of officers who are unlikely to be promoted again. It is within this context that we propose some possibilities for future consideration.[7] We aim to reduce the percentage of low-performing, long-tenured officers, whether through improved promotion screening, greater separation authorities, or circumstances that incentivize better performance from those capable of it.

First, the services may wish to use new promotion authorities to better identify officers for promotion. The FY 2019 NDAA introduced new promotion authorities that, separately or combined, might reduce the frequency with which officers are promoted beyond their capability. 10 U.S.C. 605 permits the military services to temporarily promote officers to a higher grade in some circumstances. This authority could be used to reduce the uncertainty of whether an officer will succeed at a higher grade. Officers who have pursued less-traditional career paths or have demonstrated high performance in less typical roles could be excellent candidates for temporary promotion, especially to O-5. The services could use the temporary promotion as a "trial period,"

---

[7] Each statutory or policy consideration would require extensive study prior to implementation, which is outside the scope of this study.

ensuring that the temporarily promoted officer can achieve the standards of the higher grade. Misidentification of potential becomes less costly for the service, as the service needs only to remove the officer from a position to reduce the officer back to the permanent grade.

The temporary promotion authority could be combined with the alternate promotion authority of 10 U.S.C. 649 to create a mechanism for reducing uncertainty in promotion readiness. The alternate promotion authority allows an identified competitive category to go before a promotion board up to five times. A military service could use the temporary promotion authority to promote individuals into a position at a higher grade and the alternate promotion authority to validate performance and provide permanent promotion. The advantage of such a combination is the establishment of a system through which officers can demonstrate their readiness for permanent promotion by serving in positions at the higher rank. The services could reduce their uncertainty as to whether an officer is ready to succeed at the next rank, with the flexibility to review records through a selection board many times.

Second, the services may benefit from legislation that allows them to involuntary separate officers after they have twice failed of selection to O-6 for selected competitive categories. Current statute allows officers at the rank of O-5 to serve to 28 years of service, including O-5s who have twice failed of selection to O-6. The military services might benefit from additional flexibility, including the ability to identify competitive categories that justify involuntary separation after O-5 officers twice failed of selection to O-6.

The freedom to identify some competitive categories, rather than all, would be an important consideration. Many officer communities place a premium on youth and vigor, whereas other officer communities benefit from long service. Those competitive categories with a stronger need for youthful officers might be suitable candidates for involuntary separation after being twice failed of selection. Applying the same policy to competitive categories that require additional experience risks separating officers who are still developing. In the case where an officer who is plausibly still developing, with many years of productive service ahead, and who resides in a competitive category with involuntary separation, the military service could move that officer to a different competitive category.

Third, the services may wish to increase incentives for productive officers to stay past 20 years. The possibilities listed above provide alternatives for decreasing the likelihood that a potentially stagnant officer is promoted and increasing opportunities to separate that officer if promoted. There is a special category of officers who might be defined as stagnant in promotion terms but not in development terms: the officer who is still developing but not advancing. Officers may have differing "productivity profiles," in part based on the experiential requirements of the career field (Warner, 2008, p. 19). Rostker (2015) testified that strategic intelligence might be such a field, while Warner (2008, p. 19) highlighted medical professionals and technical specialists, among others. Other career fields combine early career warfighting expertise and substantial midcareer training investments, such as foreign area officers (Parcell and Kraus, 2010, p. 44). Officers in this category might still provide valuable service to the military past the 20-year retirement cliff, but current policies provide few incentives for longer service. In Appendix E (Robbert et al., 2021), we present analysis of the separation trends of O-5s in combat and noncombat specialties, which found no broad differences between the two groups.

One potential approach to increasing incentives would be to increase the quality of job matches for officers of long tenure. In Appendix D (Robbert et al., 2021), we modeled a scenario in which an officer retires from the service when the level of perceived performance—or how productive the service thinks an officer is—departs significantly below the true level of capability for an officer. An important finding from our model is that officers of higher talent will depart at a higher rate than less talented peers, which in turn lowers the aggregate talent level of officers who remain. Increasing the probability that an officer of long tenure will be matched to an appropriate job might increase the retention rate of high-quality officers of long tenure. Officers of lower quality might also remain at higher rates as well, but other separation authorities could be applied.

Another potential incentive, which is expanded below in the issue area on contracts, is contractually guaranteed stabilization at an agreed-upon location for officers who possess certain skills and quality markers. Officers past 20 years of service face many interconnected challenges: building up home equity, older children preparing for high school or college, or a spouse approaching peak earning years. For officers who might still provide value to the military but are unlikely to be promoted again, a contract that provides stabilization in exchange for additional years of service might be a valuable, targeted tool to retain quality officers late in a military career.

Other Considerations

Blended Retirement System Effects

The BRS might influence officer retention. It is the most significant reform of the military retirement system since World War II (Asch, Mattock, and Hosek, 2017, p. 1). BRS adds matching contributions to the Thrift Savings Plan and a lump-sum continuation pay (CP) to a reduced defined benefit payment. As with the legacy retirement system, service members qualify for the defined benefit pension upon 20 years of service.

The matching contribution feature of BRS adds an agency contribution to the service member's Thrift Savings Plan account, up to 5 percent of basic pay. The matching contribution ends when the service member reaches 26 years of service. As a result, service members at or beyond 26 years of service will not quality for matching payments, which, in turn, creates a disincentive for long careers (Thrift Savings Plan, 2017).

The CP feature of BRS provides the services with a mechanism for adjusting retention rates of midcareer personnel (both officer and enlisted). CP is paid as a multiple of basic monthly pay, in a range between 2.5 and 13 times basic monthly pay for the AC and between 0.5 and six times basic monthly pay for the RC. The services can target specific populations and use CP to meet "service-specific retention needs, specialty skills and hard-to-fill positions" (DoD Office of Financial Readiness, 2017, p. 19).

Recent RAND research (Asch, Mattock, and Hosek, 2017) suggests that CP multiples might influence retention. Using the Dynamic Retention Model, the research team modeled an individual's retention decisions over the course of the career. "The DRM accounts for expected military and external earnings, allows for individual differences in their taste for military service and for random shocks in each period, and permits the individual to reoptimize depending on the conditions realized in a period" (Asch, Mattock, and Hosek, 2017, p. xi). While the baseline multiple of 2.5 met historic retention standards for the enlisted AC force, the same 2.5 multiple fell short of historic officer retention. The research team optimized the CP to match historic officer retention and found that a multiple between nine and 13 would be needed, depending on the service (Asch, Mattock, and Hosek, 2017, p. 22).

The full effects of BRS will not be known for years. At this writing, each of the services employs the baseline 2.5 multiple for the AC (DoD, 2019). Relatively few officers will be eligible for CP for several years, as currently serving officers had the option to join BRS and few did. A low multiple might discourage retention well before officers reach 20 years of service. In such a scenario, fewer officers will reach the limits of their promotion potential and potential stagnancy, if only because there are fewer officers across the quality spectrum.

Another consideration is that abnormally high promotion opportunities might contribute to longer careers in some cases. In Figures 4.1 and 4.2, we show that the Army experienced a higher rate of officer retention at the grade of O-5. The Army also had greater promotion opportunity,[8] and often significantly so, than the other services in the late 2000s, and the rate exceeded 100 percent for five consecutive years (2006–2010) in its largest competitive category. In 2008, for example, the promotion opportunity to O-5 ranged from 100 percent to 117 percent for the Army's three primary competitive categories (Department of the Army, Office of the Deputy Chief of Staff G-1, 2009); this was substantially above the rate in the predominant competitive categories of the other services (Department of the Air Force, undated; Department of the Navy, 2009b; Department of the Navy, 2009c).

We calculated the "survival rate" of O-5s in the Army, which is the rate at which an officer will remain in the service at the same grade years into the future. In Figure 4.3, we compared the survival rate for Army O-5s from the twentieth year of service with the twenty-fourth year of service and compared the rate by source of commission. O-5s who do not "survive" were either promoted to the next rank or retired.

---

[8] Promotion opportunity is calculated by dividing the total number of officers selected for promotion (in the zone, above the zone, below the zone) by the number of officers in the promotion zone.

Figure 4.3. Army O-5 Long-Term Retention Rate, 2005–2018, by Source of Commission and Percentage That Reach the Twenty-Fourth Year of Commissioned Service as an O-5

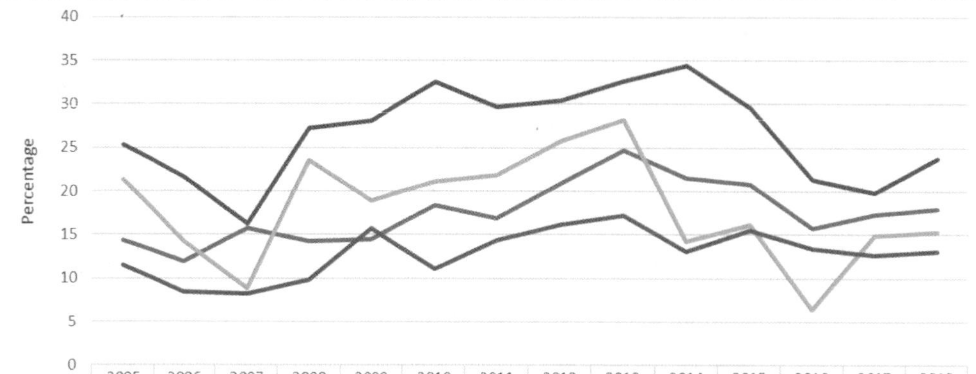

	2005	2006	2007	2008	2009	2010	2011	2012	2013	2014	2015	2016	2017	2018
ROTC scholarship program	14	12	16	14	14	18	17	21	25	22	21	16	17	18
ROTC non-scholarship program	25	22	16	27	28	32	30	30	33	34	30	21	20	24
OCS	21	14	9	24	19	21	22	26	28	14	16	6	15	15
U.S. Military Academy	11	8	8	10	16	11	14	16	17	13	16	13	13	13

The survival rate for Army O-5s originating from Officer Candidate School (OCS) or a nonscholarship Reserve Officer Training Corps (ROTC) program exceeded those from West Point or ROTC scholarship programs. These findings suggest, but do not prove, that increased promotion opportunity to O-5 might yield a higher long-term retention of officers from accessions sources with lower accession quality distributions.[9] When the Army implemented SERBs and eSERBs for O-5s in 2013 and 2014, the decline in the survival rate was greatest for the lower accession quality sources. To expand the analysis, we considered the correlation between the promotion rate and the survival rate by source of commission, as shown in Table 4.2.

[9] Gerras and Wong (2016) summarized several studies that show differences in college entrance exam scores, grade-point average requirements, and career outcomes (both early and late in a career) based on U.S. Army officer accession source.

Table 4.2. Correlation Coefficients Between Army Promotion Rate to O-5 and Survival Rate to Twenty-Fourth Year of Active Commissioned Service as O-5, by Source of Commission

Promotion Time Period[a]	U.S. Military Academy	ROTC Scholarship	ROTC Nonscholarship	OCS	All Army
2001–2011[b]	0.73	0.70	0.77	0.35	0.77
2001–2009[c]	0.73	0.68	0.76	0.51	0.76

[a] The correlation coefficients reflect the relationship between the promotion rate in a given period and the survival rate to a period four years later. For instance, the promotion period from 2001–2011 would be compared with the survival rate from 2005–2015.
[b] This period includes years before the increased promotion rate to O-5 and years during which O-5s were subject to SERB or eSERB.
[c] This period includes years before the increased promotion rate to O-5 and concludes before O-5s were subject to SERB or eSERB.

Across a variety of time frames, the promotion rate to O-5 is correlated with the survival rate to the twenty-fourth year of service as an Army O-5. The correlation is strongest for officers produced by ROTC without a scholarship. Interestingly, and unexpectedly, the correlation is *weakest* for OCS as a commissioning source. One explanation might be that OCS graduates include many with prior enlisted service; those officers would reach the twenty-fourth year of active service before the twenty-fourth year of active commissioned service.

The experience of the Army during this period—a period during which the Army dramatically increased its promotion opportunity to O-5—underscores the necessity for policy options for addressing an increased percentage of officers reaching long tenure without further promotion.

Issue: Given the Legislative Change Removing the Requirement to Achieve 20 Years of Commissioned Service by Age 62, What Controls, If Any, Could Be Put in Place?

Section 501 of the FY 2019 NDAA repealed the requirement for officers to have the ability to complete 20 years of service by age 62 as a qualification for an original appointment as a regular commissioned officer (Public Law 115-232). In practice, the removal of the age restriction will allow the services to commission officers with more advanced nonmilitary experience in order to fulfill requirements. While officers in most career fields are still required to retire by age 62, the provision enables individuals over the age of 42 to commission as officers. The main limitations to the use of commissioning age controls involve cultural and fiscal constraints, as indicated in Table 4.3.

The new authority is bolstered by Section 502 of the FY 2019 NDAA, which enhances the "availability of constructive service credit for private sector training or experience upon original appointment as a commissioned officer." The provision expands upon a previous authority that allowed for constructive credit through the grade of O-4; the new authority allows for constructive credit up to the grade of O-6. While Sections 501 and 502 (the removal of the age restriction and the allowance of constructive credit through the grade of O-6) should not be conflated with one another, they mutually reinforce one another. The services will now be able to access a previously untapped talent pool (older individuals with vast private-sector experience) and provide them with a commensurate rank and pay grade.

This flexibility complements the creation of BRS. While the traditional retirement system required 20 years of service to access an individual's retirement benefits, BRS enables individuals with less than 20 years of service to access a portion of their retirement benefits. As a result, the services can now provide an additional recruiting incentive to competitive individuals to meet requirements.

Table 4.3. Commissioning Age Controls

	Constraints?			
Domain	**Yes**	**No**	**Comments**	**Mitigation Strategy**
Statutory		X	The FY 2019 NDAA lifted the previous statutory limitations on age at time of commissioning (previous limitation was age 42).	
Policy		X		Current policies enable chaplains and other professional career fields to defer retirement to age 68, which could be modeled for other career fields.
Cultural	X		Organization places an emphasis on a "young and vigorous" force.	
			Officers who commission at older ages—and, particularly, those who are lateral entries at higher grades—may have less service culture awareness.	DoD and/or the services can clearly define required military training in order to provide service credibility for senior lateral commissions.
			There are potential for morale/retention/promotion pipeline problems in system if officers over age 42 commission above the grade of O-1 via lateral entry.	Limit the number of officers over age 42 commissioned via lateral entry.
Fiscal	X		There are possible cost implications if retirement benefits are earned with less than 20 years of services (but it is not a significant factor if numbers are small).	The implementation of BRS enables those with shorter careers to retire with some benefits without serving a 20-year career.
			There are potential force-planning challenges if older lateral entry officers have shorter, more senior career paths.	Force planning in key career fields (such as cyber) can account for the likelihood and/or number of older lateral entry officers.

Constraints

Statutory

Section 502 of the FY 2019 NDAA removes a previous constraint in 10 U.S.C. 532, requiring individuals be able to serve 20 years on active duty before age 62 (limiting accessions at age 42).

Under Section 502, the retirement age remains 62, but individuals are able to commission at ages older than 42 and younger than 62.

Policy

Current policy does not restrict the services' ability to commission officers over the age of 42. Historically, certain career fields, such as medical doctors and chaplains, have commissioned older officers with more professional experience; these career fields may provide the services with a model of how to access and utilize individuals with significant professional experience to meet service requirements. Existing law enables officers within these professional career fields to defer retirement until age 68 (10 U.S. Code 1251). In both of these communities, the service secretaries make the determination as to whether the officer may defer their retirement until age 68, with the recognition that the service benefits from the professional officer's experience and the ability to meet the service's requirements.

Cultural

The largest potential constraints to implementation of the new authority are cultural. The Officer Personnel Act, passed in 1947, cited the need for a "young and vigorous force" as one of the three main priorities for personnel reform. In testimony before the Senate Armed Services Committee, General Eisenhower, then the Chief of Staff of the Army, stated the need to "replace" older, stagnant officers from command positions and to keep "the outflow at the top so as to keep your vigorous body underneath" (U.S. Senate, 1947). Therefore, there may be a cultural aversion to commissioning officers at older ages. Also, the age constraint was more than likely associated with ensuring 20 years of commissioned service prior to an officer being involuntarily retired at age 62.

Another cultural concern relates to the combination of the new commissioning age controls and lateral entry. If a large number of officers above the age of 42 commission in grades above O-1, there is a potential for stagnation in the system, which in turn could lead to morale issues and ultimately retention problems.

Fiscal

The new provision may face fiscal constraints, as individual officers with less than 20 years of active duty service will be able to retire with some portion of their retirement benefits through BRS. However, the number of individuals commissioning at older ages is likely to be small and focused within technical fields. Therefore, we do not project a significant increase in costs upon implementation.

Service Perspectives

The services provided varying perspectives on the use of the new authority. The Army, Navy, and Air Force expressed an openness to utilizing the new authority for certain technical career paths but did not anticipate using the authority for more traditional command paths (particularly those in the combat arms or line positions). The Marine Corps representative indicated that the Marine Corps has no intention of using the new authority. The Marine Corps perspective is consistent with its overall views on lateral entry; because the Marine Corps values the shared experience of the traditional career path and its associated training, it does not intend to allow individuals to commission as officers through lateral entry. Further, the Marine Corps differs from the other services in its approach to professional career fields, as it does not commission its own medical professionals (relying on the Navy to provide the requirement instead). The difference in approach is consistent with an emphasis on a shared traditional career path.

Proposed Way Forward

The services can consider the career fields and conditions under which it is preferable to access older officers. Interviews with the military departments suggest that certain career fields may benefit from commissioning older officers with more professional experience, to include logistics, cyber, and acquisitions. To prevent promotion pipeline and retention problems, an incremental approach may be most appropriate. The departments may wish to start with the accession of small numbers of older lateral entries within a single competitive category to measure the impacts and then adjust as necessary. The military departments may also wish to avoid a demonstration that combines the use of the new commissioning age controls and lateral entry with any other reforms that have the potential to create stagnation in the current system if adopted too broadly, such as the alternative promotion authority.

Additionally, the services place an emphasis on the value of shared training and experience among more senior officer grades. While officers commissioning at older ages are more likely to enter career fields that would benefit from their technical proficiency (i.e., cyber) or comparable skills from the private sector (i.e., logistics and acquisitions) than combat arms career fields, they may still face cultural disadvantages vis-à-vis their peers. To mitigate this, the services could set forth clear policy on the training required for officers accessing at older ages and consider ways in which training should acculturate older accessions to military culture and experience. The services could further clearly define the types of positions in which older officers will be accessed and the requirements these officers must meet.

Other Considerations

Another consideration is the evolution of civilian workforce dynamics, which may lead to the potential appeal of a military career later in life. The military retirement age was initially set at 62 in order to maintain the military's competitiveness as an employer as compared with civil service and the private sector (Kamarck, 2018). Changes in retirement systems within the private sector, particularly the shift from defined benefit retirement systems (pensions) to defined contribution retirement systems (i.e., 401K programs) are shifting individuals' decisions regarding when to retire (Military Compensation and Retirement Modernization Commission, 2015). Further, changes in life expectancies and the nature of work are leading to increases in the length of careers, whether by choice or necessity (Toossi and Torpey, 2017). It is therefore possible that the services could benefit from the experience of individuals who did not consider the military for their first career but are open to bringing their expertise to work in the military.

Section 502 of the FY 2019 NDAA still maintains that individuals will be involuntarily retired at age 62. However, whereas the previous statute limited officer accessions past the age of 42, the new provision would enable older individuals with greater private or public sector experience to commission at any age prior to 62 years of age. The change could impact throughput in several ways. First, the removal of the requirement to be able to serve 20 years before mandatory retirement at age 62 would shorten the length of certain officers' careers. For example, an individual commissioning at age 58 would be able to serve for only four years before reaching their mandatory age of retirement. The services need to consider how shorter, more senior careers would therefore be managed. Second, as discussed above, the introduction of shorter careers in combination with lateral entry at more senior grades may have implications for the promotion potential of officers in more junior grades.

Issue: What Statutory and Policy Changes Are Required for Officers to Be Contracted the Way That Enlisted Members Are Today, and What Are the Pros and Cons of Doing So?

Discussions with the sponsor indicated an interest in examining whether there might be any benefits to considering how officers might be contracted similarly to the way enlisted service members are currently managed. A contracting system might be used to enable the extension of careers for high-tenure competitive officers or to assist the services in meeting requirements where shortfalls currently exist. The following section addresses the statutory and policy changes required to contract officers as enlisted members are contracted and highlights what the advantages and challenges of such contracts would be. Key issues are highlighted in Table 4.4.

Table 4.4. Contracted Service for Officers

Domain	Constraints? Yes	Constraints? No	Comments	Mitigation Strategy
Statutory	X		Title 10 requires a board or show-cause for officer separation.	Create explicit statutory provision for contracted term of service with specified renewal options.
Policy	X		DoDI 1310.02 requires that "only those persons who have clearly demonstrated the potential for *full careers* will be appointed as military officers to sustain the quality and effectiveness of the force" (p. 1) (emphasis added).	DoD can remove the requirement for full-career potential.
			There is concern that officer reaction might be to sue military departments for contract violations.	Keep contracts broad (similar to enlisted contracts), addressing only tenure, but not putting specific limits on permanent change of station (PCS) and TDY deployments, or other specific obligations.
Cultural	X		Cultural aversion to using contracts for the officer profession exists.	Consider the current systems in place for enlisted service members and the effectiveness of those systems.
Fiscal	X		The practice could extend careers of experienced senior officers in higher pay grades.	Account for high-tenure senior officers in the personnel budget process and consider the return on investment for retaining skills and experience as compared with accessing and developing new officers to meet requirements.

Currently, the services access officers and enlisted service members through two distinct avenues. Enlisted service members enter the service through enlistment contracts, stipulated in 10 U.S.C. 505 as a period of between two and eight years of service for all individuals with less than ten years of service prior to enlistment or reenlistment. Individuals reenlisting with at least ten years of service may reenlist for either a specified period of time between two and eight years or an unspecified period of time. By contrast, officers are commissioned under the authority of 10 U.S.C. 531–541.

The services currently have mechanisms in place operating similar to contracts: active duty service obligations. While these can be used to ensure minimum periods of service, they cannot function the way a contract would to potentially limit tenure.

Constraints

There are two ways in which the services could utilize a contracted model for officers. The first application is a contract model for all officers throughout the length of their career. The second application is a contract model to retain high-tenure, competitive officers and terminate stagnant officers. Either application would require both statutory and policy change.

Statutory

Current statute limits the ability of the services to contract officers in the way enlisted service members are contracted today. While a commission is associated with a minimum required time in service, it does not provide a maximum time in service short of retirement or the convening of a board for the specific purpose of separating officers. As noted under the stagnant officer section above, Title 10 requires a board or show-cause for officer separation. 10 U.S.C. 638 provides for SERB. 10 U.S.C. 647 provides for force-shaping boards. Therefore, under current statute, officers could not be involuntarily separated from service without the use of a board or for cause, which, in turn, hinders the use of a contract system for officers (particularly for service members of shorter tenure).

Policy

In policy, DoDI 1310.02, *Appointing Commissioned Officers*, requires that "only those persons who have clearly demonstrated the potential for full careers will be appointed as military officers to sustain the quality and effectiveness of the force" (p. 1). While this DoDI does not define the terms of "potential for a full career," they are largely understood as the potential to promote through the ranks over the course of a career toward retirement at 20 years of service or more. In order to implement a contract system for officers, DoDI would need to be updated to remove the requirement for a full career at the time of commissioning.

Cultural

Culturally, there is a perception that the professionalism of the officer corps could be hindered by a contract model (if applied to all officers for the length of their career). Enlisted (specifically junior enlisted) service members can be contracted for their technical proficiency, but officers carry the constitutional authority required to execute the will of the state (Huntington, 1957). The weight of a commission's authority and responsibility creates a system in which "professionalism" is associated with the ability to serve a full career as a commissioned officer.

Within the general officer corps, cultural expectations effectively operate as contracts. For example, within the Marine Corps, each officer promoted to the grade of O-7 (brigadier general) is expected to provide a letter of intent to retire to the Commandant of the Marine Corps at the time of his or her promotion in order to "promote the steady promotion flow" of future general officers (Department of the Navy, 2015). Marine Corps generals are expected to submit their letter of intent to retire at two years TIG, effective upon reaching three years TIG. The Commandant of the Marine Corps reserves the right to execute the requested retirement or return the letter to the officer without action or upon the general officer's promotion to the next grade. The system effectively serves as a contract, providing the minimum TIG required to retire (three years) while also providing a maximum TIG if the letter of intent to retire is executed.

Fiscal

Personnel costs could be affected if the policy were to shift the seniority distribution of the force. Increased retention of high-tenure officers could reduce the need for new accessions, thereby increasing the number of high-tenure senior officers and reducing the number of low-tenure junior officers.

Service Perspectives

Discussions with service representatives indicate a lack of interest in using contracted terms for officers similar to those used for enlisted service members. First, service representatives noted that senior enlisted members (those with over ten years of service) are currently managed through indefinite contracts, meaning that as an enlisted service member enters the ranks of professional noncommissioned officers, they are managed more like officers. The services therefore questioned the utility of managing officers in a manner similar to that through which junior enlisted service members' careers are managed. Second, the services were concerned that the types of terms an officer might desire in order to sign a contract (for example, a specific location or unit assignment) may not be feasible. The result would either be an insufficient incentive for an officer to sign a contract or may open the service up to potential lawsuits if terms are breached. Lastly, service representatives raised concerns regarding the attractiveness of a contract model for high-performing, long-tenure officers. Such officers may be willing to remain on active duty for an additional year but may choose to retire if their options are either to retire or sign a contract for an extended period of time (for example, three years). In those cases, the service benefits from retaining the officer for one additional year rather than losing him or her to retirement.

The services are generally not interested in executing a contract model for officers. First, the services expressed a concern that extending a contract model to the officer corps may lead to lawsuits if the service is unable to meet any contracted incentives therein (such as guaranteed locations). In order to mitigate concern over potential lawsuits, officer contracts would need to be kept broad (much like enlisted contracts), addressing only tenure, but not PCS, TDY deployments, or other specific service obligations.

Additionally, the services express concern that contracts for more competitive, experienced officers would disincentivize continued service. Individuals with high tenure who may be willing to extend their careers for a short period of time (for example, one to three more years on active service) may choose to leave the service altogether if their only option is to sign a contract for a longer period of service (for example, five more years of service).

Proposed Way Forward

If the services see utility in contracted terms, they would need to submit a legislative proposal explicitly authorizing contracted periods of service. The statute should address contract renewal options open to both the service and the individual. Those separated due to nonrenewal of a contract would, presumably, be exempted from the requirement for a SERB or show-cause action for officer separation.

Within policy, DoD can remove the requirement for an officer to have the potential to serve a full career from the applicable DoDI.

5. Other Issues

This chapter discusses three issues that did not fit into either of the categories—promotions and tenure—covered in the previous two chapters:

- Given a common retirement system for active and reserve personnel and the anticipated alignment of benefits under the duty-status reform initiative, what is still missing to provide for continuum of service/permeability (switching components at will)?
- What legislation is necessary for all services to have WOs and LDOs?
- Could an "officers without rank" concept provide additional flexibility for technical and traditional officer career tracks (e.g., medical, legal, cyber, acquisition, or others)?

Issue: Given a Common Retirement System for Active and Reserve Personnel and the Anticipated Alignment of Benefits Under the Duty Status Reform Initiative, What Is Still Missing to Provide for Continuum of Service/Permeability (Switching Components at Will)?

DoD RCs' evolution from a strategic force to an operational force derives primarily from shifts in the strategic environment. The aftermath of 9/11 led to an increase in the demand for U.S. military forces to project U.S. power around the globe and the emergence of the RCs as an operational force. Along with this evolution has come the need to develop personnel policies that manage the active and RCs as an integrated total force. This began with an initiative to implement a "continuum of service" (Commission on the National Guard and Reserves, 2008). Such a continuum of service was meant to "ease the seamless transition of individual reservists on and off active duty to meet mission requirements over the course of their military careers" (Commission on the National Guard and Reserves, 2008, p. 136). Later, the concept of *permeability* between the active and reserve components was part of DoD's FOTF personnel reform initiative announced in 2015.

As part of these various efforts to further integrate the active and reserve components, DoD established a BRS for both active- and reserve-component members. In addition, DoD has been mandated by Congress to reform the current reserve-component duty status in order to minimize disruptions in pay and benefits as reserve-component members transition from the RC to the AC—including transitioning from Title 32 and Title 10 status. By significantly streamlining the reserve-component duty-status system, those transitions should become much less disruptive. However, there are other enhancements that could be made to enhance the seamless transition between the active and reserve components. These enhancements are discussed below. Considerations are summarized in Table 5.1.

Table 5.1. Additional Enhancements for Active/Reserve Permeability

	Constraints?			
Domain	**Yes**	**No**	**Comments**	**Mitigation Strategy**
Statutory	X		Traditional Terms and Conditions of Service constrain movement across components.	Change Terms and Conditions of Service to allow for more flexibility across components.
			Scrolling process is required.	Streamline or eliminate the scrolling process. (Several legislative proposals are being considered.)
			Current 1,095-day strength accounting requirement potentially constrains volunteerism.	Clarify 1,095-day requirement and limitations on full-time support (FTS) duties.
			There is confusion over legal limitations on duties that FTS personnel may perform.	Provide RC chiefs and secretary concerned with greater flexibility in determining missions that FTS personnel may perform.
			Separate officer management systems.	Consider whether this should be a long-term goal and consider a phased transition to a single personnel management system.
Policy	X		Separate pay and benefits systems.	Continue to support development of integrated pay and personnel systems (IPPS).
			Current career development paths are prescriptive and rigid; therefore, they do not easily lend themselves to cross-component talent management strategies.	Incentivize cross-component assignments; analyze feasibility and career progression implications if cross-component assignments could count for joint time.
Cultural	X		There is cultural distrust and lack of understanding of each component's skills, capabilities, and strengths.	Continue to experiment with cross-component pilot programs.
Fiscal	X		Separate pots of funding for RC (Reserve Personnel Appropriations [RPA]) and AC (Military Personnel Appropriations [MPA]).	Align fiscal and personnel resources.

Constraints

Statutory changes could facilitate permeability by providing more flexibility in authorities and funding. Policy changes could incentivize service members to participate in cross-component assignments to gain a better understanding of both the active and reserve components and their respective capabilities, as well as break down cultural distrust across the components. In addition, providing more budget flexibility and aligning appropriations to personnel resources could also facility permeability.

Statutory

As mentioned earlier, one of the biggest barriers to transitioning across components is the enormously complicated reserve-component duty-status system, which is comprised of about 30 duty statuses. Service members regularly move from one duty-status to another depending on factors such as the mission, type of mobilization, the type of orders they receive, and the type of funding for the mobilization. Moving between these various statuses, including between Title 10 (active duty) and Title 32 (full-time National Guard duty) can cause major disruptions in pay and benefits for service members. Recent ongoing efforts to streamline the current duty-status system will hopefully address the problems associated with the current system, and it will also allow for a more seamless transition across the active and reserve components (both the Reserves and the National Guard).

Traditional terms and conditions of service (e.g., the length of service obligation, requiring full-time service for the length of the service obligation) can also be a barrier to permeability and developing a career that is comprised of both full-time and part-time service. There is also some concern that potential military recruits may not be interested in traditional terms and conditions of service (e.g., they may not want to serve the traditional length of a full-time active duty contract and instead may want to work part-time in the military, with the flexibility of moving to full-time as their life circumstances change). If these terms and conditions of service allowed more flexibility to move across components, permeability could be facilitated.

The U.S. military is also looking to examples in foreign militaries to see how they have dealt with the same challenges. For instance, the Australian Defence Force (ADF) has come up with some novel approaches to permeability. ADF faces similar permeability barriers and has been working on a plan to "develop a contemporary employment model with associated conditions of service based on the concept of an ADF career for life, particularly to allow permanents to move seamlessly to part time work in their work/life balance and for reservists to move seamlessly to full time work in the ADF" (Defence Reserves Association Submission, 2015, p. 11). The Australian military is also implementing a "Total Workforce Model" that offers improved access to flexible career options by enabling mobility across full-time and part-time service as personal circumstances change (Australian Government, undated). As discussed in Chapter 3, the scrolling process (the process of whereby officers transition from the active-duty list to the reserve active-status list or vice versa) is also perceived to be a burdensome process and a major barrier to permeability due to the time it takes to complete the process. Several legislative proposals are currently being considered to streamline or eliminate the scrolling process. As mentioned earlier in this report, there appears to be an unsettled question regarding the extent to which statutory language must be changed to permit single appointment scrolling of active and reserve appointments.[1] However, if reserve appointments for active-duty officers could be considered equivalent to appointments of officers in the RCs, these officers could move between components without the need for reappointment scrolling.

Another barrier to permeability is confusion over some strength accounting requirements and legal limitations on the utilization of particular types of personnel. By clarifying these requirements, DoD can ameliorate some of the limitations that these misconceptions create.

---

[1] *Single scrolling* means eliminating the distinction between regular and reserve appointments.

One method for clarifying requirements could be through the issuance of official guidance specifically addressing these statutory issues.

One such end-strength reporting requirement that has caused some confusion is the so called 1,095-day rule, which requires that if a service member's order specifies a period of duty greater than three years or if the member's cumulative periods of active duty and Full-Time National Guard duty exceed 1,095 days in the previous 1,460 days, than that service member must be counted in either the active-duty strength authorization or the Active Guard Reserve (AGR) end-strength authorization from the day the order specifying a period greater than three years is issued or from the 1,096th day of duty forward (10 U.S.C. 115(b)(2)). This does not preclude a service member from serving or continuing to serve on active duty or Full-Time National Guard duty to provide operational support; it is simply an end strength reporting requirement.

Confusion over the restrictions on the duties that FTS personnel may perform—both their primary duties and their additional duty—also limit the ability of the RC to use this personnel resource to provide operational support. The law delineates that the primary responsibilities for AGRs are organizing, administering, recruiting, instructing, or training of the RCs. According to DoD policy, AGRs are permitted to perform duties outside of their primary responsibilities, but those additional duties must not interfere with those responsibilities (DoDI 1205.18, 2014). However, there is some confusion over how much time AGRs can dedicate to duties other than organizing, administering, recruiting, instructing, or training, which may lead some personnel managers to believe that AGRs are not permitted to perform any other duties that they might be assigned. But this is not the case. The law also prescribes, and limits, the additional duties that AGRs are permitted to perform. One way to address this issue is to provide the Reserve component chiefs and secretaries with greater flexibility in determining missions that FTS personnel may perform.

In 2008, the Commission on the National Guard and Reserve identified a single officer management system as a long-term goal that DoD should pursue. While such a goal carries with it associated statutory and policy changes, DoD should consider whether this should be a long-term goal to facilitate increased permeability and, if so, examine ways in which such a system could be implemented through an incremental approach that would allow time for developing and analyzing measures of effectiveness related to the impact on warfighting readiness, effectiveness, and retention. To this end, the consolidation of officer management systems could begin with certain occupations/specialties, ranks, and so on.

Policy

Along the same lines, separate pay and personnel systems across the active and reserve components also serve as barriers to permeability. There are ongoing efforts across the services to establish IPPS that serve both active and reserve component members.

Another barrier to permeability is the rigidity and prescriptive nature of current career paths. While some of these issues have been addressed with recent reforms to the officer management system (see Robbert et al., 2019), additional enhancements could be made. These include (1) providing incentives for service members to take on cross-component assignments in which

AC officers are assigned to an RC unit or RC officers are assigned to an AC unit (such as the experiences described in the following section), or (2) analyzing the feasibility and implications of allowing cross-component assignments to count toward promotion requirements.

For instance, DoD could make changes to precepts and board charges to facilitate permeability. DoD could document the importance and expectation of cross-component assignments and ask board members to give "special consideration" for this experience. DoD could also specifically state that command in one component should be considered equivalent to command in another component.

DoD could also increase the number and percentage of cross-component officers on each board to foster greater understanding and appreciation for cross-component experience. This mix of board membership could reinforce an enterprise-wide perspective.

Cultural

One of the enduring barriers to permeability continues to be cultural distrust across active and reserve components, as well as a lack of understanding of each component's skills, capabilities, and strengths. This distrust across components stems from previous eras when the RC did not have much combat experience and suffered from training and readiness deficiencies. However, since 9/11, the RC has played a key role in certain warfighting missions (e.g., remotely piloted aircraft, combat support, air refueling, airlift), and the occupations/specialties have also been concentrated in the RC. As a result, active- and reserve-component members have been carrying out warfighting missions side-by-side for a prolonged time, and in some cases, they have developed a better understanding of their respective components and skill sets. However, this is not always the case. One way to break down this distrust and lack of understanding is to increase cross-component experiences so that service members have a better understanding of the strengths and weaknesses of active- and reserve-component capabilities. Ultimately, this type of cross-component experience could foster the development of officers who have a more holistic, enterprise-wide perspective of the total force.

The Army's Total Force Assignment Program (TFAP), currently at a pilot stage, provides an example of incentivizing cross-component experience. This program will provide cross-component opportunities for junior AC captains to take a two-year assignment that includes one year of training in a U.S. Army Reserve rapid call-up unit and another year in command of that U.S. Army Reserve unit.[2] The design of TFAP offers important insights for the other services because the program has deliberately tried to identify a point in AC officers' careers when they could participate in a cross-component assignment without such an assignment competing with other mandatory career requirements. The result is that TFAP will be offered to junior AC captains who have just completed the advanced course—a time when they would be conducting routine staff assignments. Thus, one of the major incentives for participating in TFAP will be the

[2] Army TFAP representative, discussion with the authors, February 22, 2017.

opportunity for junior AC captains to take a second command assignment at a point in their career when they otherwise would not have that opportunity.

Fiscal

A fiscal barrier to permeability is the separate pots of funding for RC and AC appropriations. Funding related to the training and other specific duty for the Reserves is provided by Congress through RPA. Funding for the same purposes is provided to the National Guard through National Guard Personnel Appropriations. Any task completed by a member of the RC in support of the AC is funded with MPA, which is the funding source for the AC (Dolfini-Reed and Stafford, 2010, p. 12). Thus, there is a mismatch between the personnel resource in the RCs and the funding resource in the AC. One way to solve this problem would be to align appropriations with strength authorization by authorizing an appropriate funding level of National Guard Personnel Appropriations and RPA to correspond to the number of reserve personnel authorized to be on active duty for operational support. Another option is to provide more budget flexibility across these various funding streams.

Service Perspectives

While none of the services identified permeability as a priority for officer management, there was widespread interest among the services in addressing issues related to scrolling, as well as disruptions in pay and benefits associated with changes in RC duty statuses. In addition, there were mixed views across the services about whether active- and reserve-component assignments should be counted as equivalent to one another. These views reflect the various degrees to which active- and reserve-component force structure is intertwined in the services, the frequency with which active- and reserve-component members conduct operational missions together, and varying perceptions of the proficiency of some RC members.

Proposed Way Forward

DoD's continuing support of duty-status reform and the development of IPPS across the services will foster increased permeability. In addition, the clarification of legal requirements such as the 1,095-day reporting requirement and limitations placed on the use of FTS personnel would be helpful so that there is a common understanding of these requirements. The continued experimentation with cross-component assignment pilot programs would also help enhance permeability by exposing more service members to these types of total-force experiences. Further, analyzing ways to increase budget flexibility or align appropriations with personnel resources could also facilitate increased permeability.

Issue: What Legislation Is Necessary for All Services to Have Warrant Officers and Limited Duty Officers?

Currently, the Navy and the Marine Corps have LDO programs, and all services except the Air Force have WO structures. In this section, we examine the extension of those programs to all services. Table 5.2 highlights the statutory, cultural, and fiscal constraints on the creation of LDO positions in services other than the Navy, as well as the cultural and fiscal constraints on the creation of WOs in the only service that does not currently have them: the Air Force. Because this topic addresses two distinct populations—LDOs and WOs—and because the most significant reforms required involve statutory changes, this section is divided along those lines rather than by the four categories of constraints listed in the table.

Table 5.2. Warrant Officers and Limited Duty Officers in All Services

	Constraints?			
Domain	**Yes**	**No**	**Comments**	**Mitigation Strategy**
Statutory	X (LDO)	X (WO)	Title 10 provisions uniformly authorize "secretary concerned" to establish and manage WO programs (571 through 583 for ACs, 12241 through 12244 for RCs), but some statutory provisions differ across services.	Reevaluate WO inconsistencies across services (10 U.S.C. 1305 regarding tenure, 10 U.S.C. 12008 regarding authorized strengths, 10 U.S.C. 9160—one year of active duty required for Air Force WO appointments).
			LDOs are currently authorized only for Navy and Marine Corps.	Move LDO provisions from Navy and Marine Corps subtitle of Title 10 to general military law subtitle.
			Permanent and temporary appointment provisions may be outdated.	Reconsider need for permanent and temporary LDO appointments.
Policy		X	Navy appoints reserve LDOs, although there is no specific U.S.C. provision for it.	
Cultural	X		Air Force does not see a need for an additional personnel category.	
Fiscal	X		Creation of LDOs in the Army and Air Force and WOs in the Air Force would require additional investments in personnel management systems and processes.	

Constraints

While there are no statutory barriers to the establishment of WOs in any service, including the Air Force, some legislative updates could promote a more standard approach to WO populations across the services. However, statutory changes would be required to authorize LDOs in the Army and Air Force.

Warrant Officers

Statutory provisions in Title 10 regarding WO appointment, promotion, separation, and retirement uniformly authorize the "secretary concerned" to take the necessary actions (571 through 583 for ACs, 12241 through 12244 for RCs). Thus, no legislation is needed for the Air Force, which is the only service that does not have a WO contingent, to institute one.

That said, we noted several provisions in Title 10 regarding WO management that are inconsistent across services. While standardization across services is not necessary to implement an Air Force WO program, OSD might want to propose legislation to provide consistency. The inconsistencies are:

- 10 U.S.C. 1305 contains service-specific language regarding mandatory retirement of regular WOs for length of service. The statute basically requires retirement 60 days after completing 30 years of active service but allows exceptions for Army and Navy WOs. For Army WOs, the years of service calculation includes only active service as a WO. For Navy WOs in the grade of W-5, 33 years of total active service is allowed.
- 10 U.S.C. 12008 indicates that the secretaries of the Army and the Air Force may prescribe the authorized WO strengths of the Army and Air Force Reserves, respectively, but is silent on the Navy and Marine Corps.
- Curiously, 10 U.S.C. 9160 provides that, if the Air Force were to have WOs, they would be appointed from those who have served at least one year of active duty in the Air Force. No other service has a statutory experience requirement similar to this.

Limited Duty Officers

LDO appointments are currently authorized by statute only within the Navy and Marine Corps. The key terms of the program are the following:

- Those appointed must be WOs or enlisted members in grade E-6 or above (10 U.S.C. 5589 and 5596).
- Appointments may be temporary or permanent and to either warrant or commissioned grades. Permanent appointments require at least ten years of active naval service (10 U.S.C. 5589 and 5596).
- Appointments are for duty in technical fields for which they are qualified (10 U.S.C. 5589).
- For reserve LDOs, the requirement for reserve commissioned officers to hold a baccalaureate degree in order to serve above the grade of O-2 does not apply (10 U.S.C. 12205).
- "Up or out," selective continuation, and maximum tenure provisions are similar to those of other commissioned officers, but with mandatory retirement dates based on total service rather than commissioned service. Additionally, they include provisions for reversion to enlisted or WO status in lieu of separation (10 U.S.C. 6383).

Navy practice is to require at least eight years of service for temporary appointments and to make all appointments initially temporary. Navy original appointments are in the grade of O-1 if coming from enlisted status and O-2 if coming from WO status (Department of the Navy, 2009a). The Marine Corps appoints LDOs only from WO status. Their original appointment is as permanent LDOs in the grade of O-3, requiring ten years of service as specified in 10 U.S.C. 5589 (Department of the Navy, 2006). Although there is no specific statutory basis for it, the

Navy has an LDO program in its RC (Department of the Navy, 2009a).[3] The program appears to rest on general reserve officer appointment authorities rather than specific statutory provisions.

Service Perspectives

Since the Navy is the only service that uses both temporary and permanent appointment authorities for LDOs, we sought the perspective of Department of the Navy representatives on the temporary/permanent distinction. Navy representatives indicated that this structure allows for a probationary approach to WO appointments and that there was no interest in changing it.

Air Force representatives indicated no interest in either a WO or an LDO program. Moreover, Robbert and colleagues (2018) found that use of WOs to meet pilot requirements would be disadvantageous. Similarly, Army representatives were not interested in developing an LDO program. In both cases, the dissuading factor was the need to establish a new personnel management structure for which no compelling need exists.

Proposed Way Forward

Statutory authority for LDO programs could be extended to the Army and the Air Force in several ways. To provide consistency across the services, the current provisions of 10 U.S.C. 5589 and 5596 could be moved from the Navy and Marine Corps subtitle of Title 10 into the general military law subtitle. Alternatively, LDO provisions could be added to the Army and Air Force subtitles, perhaps with provisions tailored to the specific needs of those services.

The approach that fosters consistency across services would seem to be more in line with the general tenor of officer management modernization in OSD. If legislation is drafted for this purpose, we would recommend removal of the distinction between temporary and permanent LDO appointments, just as the distinction between temporary and permanent grades for commissioned officers was removed as part of DOPMA and ROPMA reforms.

Issue: Could an "Officers Without Rank" Concept Provide Additional Flexibility for Technical and Traditional Officer Career Tracks?

Per sponsor guidance, this issue was intended to address the possibility of establishing a category of officers without rank. Reasons for considering this change would be to provide an alternate career management structure for professionals in selected disciplines where grades can detract from effectiveness. Such a change could also provide alternative paths for those interested in military service to join later in life, though some provisions already exist for lateral entry. Creating a category of officers without rank could provide greater flexibility for those with

[3] The only reference to reserve LDOs in Title 10 is in 10 U.S.C. 12205, which, as indicated in the text, pertains to baccalaureate degree requirements for reserve officers.

specialized experience who are compelled to service later in life, for example. Depending on their age, career specialty, or other factors, these individuals might currently require waivers from their service secretaries, which could subject them to a lengthy approval process. It is possible that an alternative construct such as becoming an officer without rank might alleviate some of these roadblocks, but determining how to integrate such officers into existing management structures would create its own challenges for DoD and the services.

Discussions with service personnel representatives revealed no career fields that stood to immediately benefit from the introduction of officers without rank. Even in medical disciplines, where, for example, a nurse could outrank a doctor during a surgical procedure, the hierarchy imposed by their duties is thought to provide the requisite authority for these professionals to perform their jobs.[4] OSD and the military departments would need to carefully consider the types of positions that would benefit most from using officers without rank. The fact that they are officers means they can perform combat roles civilians cannot. Officers would be protected by Geneva Conventions and held accountable under the Uniform Code of Military Justice (UCMJ).

The most likely candidates could be the professional corps—medical, legal, and chaplain—where rank is potentially less relevant to how these officers perform their duties. However, there could also be innovative ways to incorporate officers without rank into existing hierarchies. These might include WOs for services that do not already have them or even provisions for civilians in uniform. Such measures would come with numerous policy and statutory requirements, which contributes to institutional reluctance from the services to pursuing these types of ideas.

As indicated in Table 5.3, there are constraints to pursuing this approach across three of the four domains we examined.

Table 5.3. Officers Without Rank

	Constraints?			
Domain	**Yes**	**No**	**Comments**	**Mitigation Strategy**
Statutory	X		There is no current provision for grade-free officer structure.	This would require creating a statutory framework for differentiating pay based on experience, competency, or other factors.
Policy	X		Primary considerations include suitability of the proposed career fields and establishing a pay structure.	Look to civilian, Senior Executive Service (SES) structures as a model.
Cultural	X		Status could appear diminished relative to ranked officers.	Include curricula on managing officers without rank into existing commanding officer or supervisor training.
Fiscal		X	Practice could be implemented in a cost-neutral way.	

[4] RAND discussions with service personnel representatives, August 2019.

Constraints

Statutory

Existing statutes from Title 10 provide for credit from prior service or allow the President and/or Secretary of Defense to appoint someone to a rank based on prior experience, but not to an unranked position.

- Section 533, "service credit upon original appointment as a commissioned officer," states that anyone receiving an original appointment will receive credit for prior active commissioned service and that those with relevant educational qualifications or specialized training can receive constructive credit for that education (10 U.S.C. 533, 2018).
- Section 12207, "commissioned officers: service credit upon original appointment," allows credit for prior service when determining what an officer's rank should be at the time of original appointment (10 U.S.C. 12207, 2018).
- Title 10, section 603, "appointments in time of war or national emergency," allows for presidential appointment of a qualified individual to an officer grade without prior service in a time of war, up to the rank of major general or rear admiral (10 U.S.C. 603, 1991). However, this statute provides for lateral entry of an individual to a particular rank, not an unranked officer.

Our research did not uncover any current provisions for incorporating officers without rank into military service. Legislative action would be required to include such a statute. A new statutory framework would need to consider whether to differentiate pay based on experience, competency, or other factors. Further, existing laws that govern officer rank might need to be revised to account for a new class of officers without rank, or new laws might need to be developed. For example, procedures for investigation, adjudication, and potential punishments under the UCMJ are based on the rank of the person being charged. Introducing officers without rank would therefore necessitate adjustments to the UCMJ, which is defined in 10 U.S.C. Subchapter X: Punitive Articles (2018).

Furthermore, any statute that would allow DoD to have officers without rank should also include provisions for their ascension. The hiring path could be the same as for ranked officers, who receive a commission from an ROTC program or service academy. For more experienced hires, the path could be simpler if officers without rank do not require commensurate credit for equivalent time served outside the military the way that lateral entries do.

Policy

All policies that deal with officer management would need to be adapted to account for this new type of officer. Establishing a pay structure for these officers is one such area. The SES approach to tiering jobs, which somewhat influences pay setting, could serve as a model to structure pay for officers without rank. Covering a wide range of levels of responsibility, the SES was intended to be a single grade. Various agencies soon recognized that compensation and other facets of personnel management were unmanageable without some tiering within the single grade. Tiers are nonstatutory rankings of executive positions that help set pay commensurate with an individual's prior experience and performance while maintaining some pay parity across jobs of approximately equal scope or responsibility.

The General Schedule (GS) pay scale could serve as a model for a more structured approach. Under the GS system, employees in a range of professional, technical, administrative, and other positions are assigned a grade between GS-1 and GS-15 and a step level within that grade between one and ten. Grades and steps are commensurate with education and prior experience. The Office of Personnel Management and the employee's home organization set performance milestones for the employee to advance between step levels and grades (U.S. Office of Personnel Management, undated). Each of these structures would be worth further consideration when determining whether pay tiers are necessary. Further, OSD and the services should establish performance milestones to help with career advancement.

Cultural

Introducing rank-less officers into the U.S. military services—inherently hierarchical organizations—would impose cultural constraints on the services. DoD should consider how it would respond to the following issues in particular:

- **Status of nonranked officers relative to ranked officers:** Where do these new officers fit in with their ranked peers? How will their experience be perceived alongside that of combat veterans? The answer could be different for every service, specialty area, or in a joint environment and could affect the credibility of nonranked officers with senior military leaders who have risen through the traditional ranks.
- **Morale effects on those already in service:** If those already in service lose rank, it could have negative effects on their morale and potentially even cause them to leave the service.
- **Rank-less officer integration:** For new officers, some training would be required to inculcate them into the ways of military service. The services could include these individuals in existing onboarding programs that teach about military life.

Those commanding or supervising officers without rank will require some training to ensure that they understand how these individuals fit within their existing command structures and that their career progression is appropriately managed, since they could have different performance milestones than their ranked peers.

Fiscal

Introducing officers without rank could be done in a cost-neutral way. By following the well-established SES model for setting pay and step increases, DoD could institute pay structures that consider an individual's prior experience, education, specialized training, and other job-related factors when establishing their pay.

Once pay structures are decided, managing the careers of officers without rank should not have major financial implications for DoD. Those already in the military who become "rank-less" will not require training on military life. New entrants would need some training, but this training could be adapted as mentioned in the previous subsection. Training for supervisors can be adapted to include modules for how to supervise rank-less officers.

Service Perspectives

Discussions with service personnel revealed no interest in creating a category of officers without rank. The concept presented no immediately obvious solutions to policy challenges, nor did there appear to be any real advantages to the services or OSD to doing so. Further, there would be numerous policy and legal requirements and cultural implications for DoD to consider should it decide to institute a rank-less structure for officers. DoD would need to undergo a thorough review of candidate career fields that would benefit from such a change, which should include the pros and cons of doing so for the services.

Even if officers without rank are introduced into the U.S. military, they will still fall under a hierarchy in some way. Medical professionals would still fall under a chief of a surgical department, for example. Currently, the Air Force Office of Special Investigators allows its personnel to perform investigations without wearing rank, but within their career field they still maintain a rank. A truly rank-less structure would require major institutional shifts—and a justification that these shifts are necessary to improving military organizations in some way.

Proposed Way Forward

Should DoD ever become interested in pursuing an officers-without-rank construct, OSD and the services would need to conduct a comprehensive review of the career fields that stand to benefit most from creating this category, including provisions for ascension, compensation, career management, advancement, and other critical factors.

Other Considerations

Although no service representatives we spoke to believed that there is an immediate need for such a structure, creative thinking could be applied to potential uses for officers without rank. For example, flatter organizations can promote opportunities for nonmanagers to contribute to innovative or new ideas (Klein and Sorra, 1996, p. 1074). Without rank, military officers could feel more empowered to offer suggestions for improvement, which they might otherwise not be comfortable making in the presence of higher-ranking officers.

In such an environment, it is critical that these individuals be officers because they would ultimately be responsible for implementing any changes that are decided on. Individuals at every level in an organization should be involved in the discussion to provide feedback on the feasibility of new ideas and firsthand insights into potential impediments to their success (Borins, 2002, p. 467). Further, this type of so-called bottom-up innovation has occurred in militaries throughout history, even if traditional hierarchical structures have been a focus for understanding military innovation (Grissom, 2006, pp. 920–925).

Existing institutions in at least two branches of service could serve as testbeds for an officer without rank structure. In the Air Force, the Air Force Warfighting Integration Capability serves as the service's internal think tank, where close to 100 personnel perform wargaming and other analyses to examine Air Force responses to potential contingencies (Mayfield, 2019). The Air Force Research Lab focuses on developing new and innovative technologies for the service (Air Force Research Lab, undated). In the Army, the new Army Futures Command was stood up in 2018 to drive Army innovation for future warfights. To achieve that goal, the Army Futures Command accepts concept submissions for capability development ideas so as to draw on the widest possible pool of ideas (Army Futures Command, undated). These organizations, while still under a command hierarchy, are designated as hubs for new ideas in their services and as such, could be amenable to introducing new officer structures if these structures promote greater idea generation. However, since military personnel assigned to these functions are expected to bring conventional military experience to bear, officers would have to transition from the ranked structure in which they gained that experience. A later transition back to a ranked system would be difficult to manage.

Further, the Commissioned Corps of the U.S. Public Health Service could provide lessons for DoD should it decide to introduce a new pathway for officers with specialized experience who become interested in military service later in their careers. While U.S. Public Health Service officers do wear a rank, they are considered a nonmilitary uniformed service, and their officers are not trained in arms (U.S. Department of Health and Human Services, undated). Rather, these officers are strictly focused on promoting public health and preventing disease. They come from a range of disciplines, including doctors, veterinarians, and scientific researchers. Expertise in these fields is the primary focus of their work, whereas medical professionals in the military services might shoulder additional responsibilities—particularly those who serve in combat roles. While the U.S. Public Health Service does not have a combat-oriented mandate, DoD could draw from its ascension and career management practices should DoD consider establishing an alternative pathway for introducing specialized experts into military service. The Public Health Service's training programs, including their Officer Basic Course, could provide lessons in integrating a different type of officer into DoD's existing officer management structure.

RAND also examined allied militaries to determine whether any officers without rank-like structures exist but found that some constructs might already be close to U.S. military approaches. For example, in the United Kingdom, Royal Army chaplains, once selected by a sending denomination, wear a "relative rank" of captain. This is similar to Royal Air Force chaplains, whose relative ranks are meant to honor their religious affiliation and their military service concurrently. Royal Navy chaplains are taught to adopt the rank of the person they are counseling as a way of better relating to the individual. Half of all naval chaplains' appointments are in deployable billets to promote a firsthand understanding of what servicemembers face in such roles (Naval Chaplaincy Service, undated).

Within each branch, chaplains mix religious training with military training, thereby deepening their understanding of military life while maintaining a focus on their civilian discipline. Their status as officers permits them to deploy alongside ranked officers and enlisted personnel alike so that their religious training can be grounded in battlefield realities, similar to chaplaincy in the U.S. military. However, any U.S. attempts at instituting officers without rank structure could benefit from consultation with allied military personnel to determine whether the construct could be effectively expanded for the right career fields.

6. Conclusions and Way Forward

Table 6.1 indicates that the most prevalent constraints we found on potential officer management modernization thrusts are cultural. This reflects a generally conservative approach to officer management in OSD and the military services—a sense that both military leadership and officers themselves are wary of changes for which outcomes would be uncertain. As discussed in Chapter 2, this conservatism is generally warranted and leads to incremental approaches to statutory or policy changes affecting officer management.

Table 6.1. Constraints on Potential Officer Management Modernization Thrusts

	Constraints			
Issue	**Statutory**	**Policy**	**Cultural**	**Fiscal**
Promotions				
Requirements-based promotions for technical-track competitive categories	X		X	
Differentiating promotion rates and frequencies across competitive categories			X	
Opting out of promotion consideration			X	
Reserve commissions for active duty officers[a]	X	X	X	
Promotion board guidance regarding deployability		X	X	
Tenure				
More liberal provisions for stagnant officers	X	X	X	
Commissioning age controls			X	X
Contracted service for officers	X	X	X	X
Other				
Additional enhancements for active/reserve permeability	X	X	X	X
WOs and LDOs in all services	X (LDO)		X	X
Officers without rank	X	X	X	

[a] The original issue, a return to temporary and permanent promotions, is reframed here in terms of the sponsor's interest in the use of reserve commissions for active duty officers as an aid to active/reserve component permeability.

Availability and Use of Statutory and Policy Provisions

In our discussions of each issue, where applicable, we provide specific statutory or policy changes that would be needed for furtherance of the issue. In some cases, service representatives questioned the need for or advisability of further change or recommended caution in pursuing further change. Combining these two considerations, we divided the issues into five categories, not necessarily exclusive of each other:

- Available provisions are sufficient and routinely used.
- Services are open to experimentation with available provisions.

- Services seek new statutory provisions.
- Services have little or no interest in available provisions.
- Services have little or no interest in new provisions.

Table 6.2 indicates how, in our estimation, each of the eleven issues we examined would be categorized.

Table 6.2. Categorizing Issues by Availability and Use of Statutory and Policy Provisions

Issue	Available Provisions Sufficient and Routinely Used	Services Open to Experimentation	Services Seek New Provisions	Little or No Interest in Available Provisions	Little or No Interest in New Provisions
Promotions					
Requirements-based promotions for technical-track competitive categories		X			
Differentiating promotion rates and frequencies across competitive categories	X	X			
Opting out of promotion consideration		X			
Reserve commissions for active duty officers as an aid to active/reserve component permeability[a]					X
Promotion board guidance regarding deployability	X				
Tenure					
More liberal provisions for stagnant officers			X		
Commissioning age controls					X
Contracted service for officers					X
Other					
Additional enhancements for active/reserve permeability		X	X		
WOs and LDOs in all services	X (Navy and Marine Corps)			X (Air Force—WO)	X (Army—LDO, Air Force—WO and LDO)
Officers without rank					X

[a] The original issue, a return to temporary and permanent promotions, is reframed here in terms of the sponsor's interest in the use of reserve commissions for active duty officers as an aid to active/reserve component permeability.

The Way Forward

For OSD and the services, the way forward would encompass two of the five categories—those in which the services are open to experimentation or seek new provisions—shown in Table 6.2. For the four issues in which the services are open to new experimentation—namely, requirements-based promotions for technical-track competitive categories; differentiating promotion rates and frequencies across competitive categories; opting out of promotion consideration; and additional enhancements for active/reserve permeability—the services could be encouraged to experiment with new flexibilities, always subject to the discretion of the service secretary regarding how far and fast to pursue them. For the two issues in which new provisions seem warranted and sought after by the services—more liberal provisions for stagnant officers and additional enhancements for active/reserve permeability—OSD and the services could begin or continue dialogue on legislative proposals to provide new flexibilities.

References

Adamsky, Dima, *The Culture of Military Innovation: The Impact of Cultural Factors on the Revolution in Military Affairs in Russia, the US and Israel*, Stanford, Calif.: Stanford University Press, 2010.

Air Force Research Lab, "About," webpage, undated. As of September 29, 2019: https://afresearchlab.com/about/

Allison, Graham, and Morton Halperin, "Bureaucratic Politics: A Paradigm and Some Policy Implications," *World Politics*, Vol. 24, No. 40, 1974, pp. 40–79.

Allison, Graham, and Philip Zelikow, *Essence of Decision*, 2nd ed., New York: Longman, 1999.

Army Futures Command, "Who We Are," webpage, undated. As of September 29, 2019: https://armyfuturescommand.com/#looking

Asch, Beth J., Michael G. Mattock, and James Hosek, *The Blended Retirement System: Retention Effects and Continuation Pay Cost Estimates for the Armed Services*, Santa Monica, Calif.: RAND Corporation, RR-1887-OSD, 2017. As of August 8, 2019: https://www.rand.org/pubs/research_reports/RR1887.html

Asch, Beth J., and John T. Warner, "A Theory of Compensation and Personnel Policy in Hierarchical Organizations with Application to the United States Military," *Journal of Labor Economics*, Vol. 19, No. 3, July 2001, pp. 523–562.

Australian Government, Department of Defence, "ADF Total Workforce Model," webpage, undated. As of March 13, 2020: https://www.defence.gov.au/ADF-totalworkforcemodel/

Bensahel, Nora, and David Barno, "First Steps Toward the Force of the Future," War on the Rocks, December 1, 2015. As of March 13, 2020: https://warontherocks.com/2015/12/first-steps-towards-the-force-of-the-future/

Borins, Sanford, "Leadership and Innovation in the Public Sector," *Leadership and Organization Development Journal*, Vol. 23, No. 8, 2002, pp. 467–476.

Cancian, Mark F., and Todd Harrison, "The Force of the Future," Washington, D.C.: Center for Strategic and International Studies, November 19, 2015. As of March 13, 2020: https://www.csis.org/analysis/force-future

Carnazza, Joseph P., Abraham K. Korman, Thomas P. Ference, and James A. F. Stoner, "Plateaued and Non-Plateaued Managers: Factors in Job Performance," *Journal of Management*, Vol. 7, No. 2, 1981, pp. 7–25.

Carson, Brad, "How We're Planning the Biggest Personnel Overhaul in 45 Years," *Defense One*, June 8, 2015. As of March 13, 2020: https://www.defenseone.com/ideas/2015/06/how-were-planning-biggest-personnel-overhaul-45-years/114733/

———, "You Don't Get to the NDAA Personnel Reforms Without Force of the Future," War on the Rocks, August 13, 2018. As of March 13, 2020: https://warontherocks.com/2018/08/you-dont-get-to-the-ndaa-personnel-reforms-without-force-of-the-future/

Carter, Phillip, Katherine Kidder, Amy Schafer, and Andrew Swick, "AVF 4.0: The Future of the All-Volunteer Force," Washington, D.C.: Center for New American Security, March 28, 2017. As of March 13, 2020: https://www.cnas.org/publications/reports/avf-4-0-the-future-of-the-all-volunteer-force

Christenson, Clayton M., and Michael Overdorf, "Meeting the Challenge of Disruptive Change," *Harvard Business Review*, March–April 2000. As of March 13, 2020: https://hbr.org/2000/03/meeting-the-challenge-of-disruptive-change

Commission on the National Guard and Reserves, *Transforming the National Guard and Reserves into a 21st Century Operational Force*, Washington, D.C.: 2008. As of April 10, 2020: https://policy.defense.gov/portals/11/Documents/hdasa/references/CNGR%20Final%20Report.pdf

Defence Reserves Association Submission, *Defence White Paper 2015*. As of March 13, 2020: https://www.defence.gov.au/WhitePaper/docs/205-DefenceReservesAssociation.pdf

Defense Entrepreneurs Forum, April 2018.

Department of the Air Force, *FY08 Active Duty Commissioned Officer Promotion Report*, Washington, D.C.: Department of the Air Force, undated.

Department of the Air Force Instruction 36-2406, *Officer and Enlisted Evaluation Systems*, November 8, 2016. As of April 16, 2019: https://static.e-publishing.af.mil/production/1/af_a1/publication/afi36-2406/afi36-2406.pdf

Department of the Army, *FY20 Colonel Army Competitive Category (ACC) Centralized Selection List (CSL)—Command/Key Billet Boards*, MILPER Message 18-207, Fort Knox, Ky.: U.S. Army Human Resources Command, July 3, 2018.

———, Army Directive 2019-30, *Authority for Officers to Opt Out of Promotion Selection Board Consideration*, Washington, D.C.: Department of the Army, 2019. As of April 10, 2020: https://armypubs.army.mil/epubs/DR_pubs/DR_a/pdf/web/ARN19445_AD2019_30_FINAL.pdf

Department of the Army, Office of the Deputy Chief of Staff G-1, *Fiscal Year 2008 Commissioned Officer Promotion Reports*, Washington, D.C.: Department of the Army, 2009.

———, *Fiscal Year 2013 Commissioned Officer Promotion Reports*, Washington, D.C.: Department of the Army, 2013.

———, *Fiscal Year 2018 Commissioned Officer Promotion Reports*, Washington, D.C.: Department of the Army, 2018.

Department of Defense Instruction 1205.18, *Full-Time Support to the Reserve Components*, Washington, D.C.: Department of Defense, 2014.

Department of Defense Instruction 1310.02, *Appointing Commissioned Officers*, Washington, D.C.: Department of Defense, 2015. As of March 30, 2020: https://www.esd.whs.mil/Portals/54/Documents/DD/issuances/dodi/131002p.pdf

Department of Defense Instruction 1320.13, *Commissioned Officer Promotion Program Reports (COPRs)*, Washington, D.C.: Department of Defense, October 30, 2014. As of March 30, 2020: https://www.esd.whs.mil/Portals/54/Documents/DD/issuances/dodi/132013p.pdf

Department of Defense Instruction 1320.14, *Commissioned Officer Promotion Program Procedures*, Washington, D.C.: Department of Defense, December 11, 2013, Incorporating Change 2, effective March 13, 2019. As of April 30, 2019: https://www.esd.whs.mil/Portals/54/Documents/DD/issuances/dodi/132014p.pdf?ver=2019-03-13-131354-800

Department of Defense Instruction 1332.18, *Disability Evaluation System*, Washington, D.C.: Department of Defense, August 5, 2014, Incorporating Change 1, effective May 17, 2018. As of May 8, 2019: https://www.esd.whs.mil/Portals/54/Documents/DD/issuances/dodi/133218p.pdf?ver=2018-05-24-133105-050

Department of Defense Instruction 1332.45, *Retention Determinations for Non-Deployable Service Members*, Washington, D.C.: Department of Defense, July 30, 2018. As of August 31, 2018: http://www.esd.whs.mil/Portals/54/Documents/DD/issuances/dodi/133245p.pdf?ver=2018-08-01-080044-667

Department of the Navy, *Marine Corps Limited Duty Officer and Warrant Officer Programs, Promotions, and Continuation Procedures*, SECNAV Instruction 1412.9B, Washington, D.C.: Department of the Navy, February 7, 2006. As of February 6, 2019: https://www.marines.mil/Portals/59/Publications/SECNAVINST%201412.9B.pdf

———, *Enlisted to Officer Commissioning Programs Application Administrative Manual*, OPNAV Instruction 1420.1B, Washington, D.C.: Department of the Navy, December 14, 2009a. As of February 6, 2019: https://www.usna.edu/Admissions/_files/documents/Fleet/OPNAVINST.pdf

———, *FY08 Commissioned Officer Promotion Reports*, Washington, D.C.: Department of the Navy, 2009b.

———, *FY08 United States Marine Corps Commissioned Officer Promotion Report*, Washington, D.C.: Department of the Navy, 2009c.

———, *Green Letter No. 1-15*, Washington, D.C.: Department of the Navy, 2015.

———, *Promotion Selection Board Deferment of Consideration for the FY-21 Promotion Selection Boards for Unrestricted Line Officers*, NAVADMIN 228/19, Washington, D.C.: Department of the Navy, 2019a. As of March 30, 2019: https://www.public.navy.mil/bupers-npc/reference/messages/Documents/NAVADMINS/NAV2019/NAV19228.txt

———, 38th Commandant of the Marine Corps, *Commandant's Planning Guidance*, Washington, D.C.: Department of the Navy, 2019b. As of September 27, 2019: https://www.hqmc.marines.mil/Portals/142/Docs/%2038th%20Commandant%27s%20Planning%20Guidance_2019.pdf?ver=2019-07-16-200152-700

DoD—*See* U.S. Department of Defense.

DoDI—*See* Department of Defense Instruction.

Dolfini-Reed, Michelle, and Darlene E. Stafford, *Identifying Duty Status Reforms Needed to Support an Operational Reserve*, Alexandria, Va.: Center for Naval Analysis, September 2010.

Evans, Lee, and Ki-Hwan Bae, "Simulation-Based Analysis of a Forced Distribution Performance Appraisal System," *Journal of Defense Analytics and Logistics*, Vol. 1, No. 2, 2017, pp. 120–136.

Freedman, Lawrence, *Strategy: A History*, Oxford: Oxford University Press, 2013.

Gerras, Stephen, and Leonard Wong, "America's Army: Measuring Quality Soldiers and Quality Officers," War on the Rocks, April 13, 2016. As of December 16, 2019: https://warontherocks.com/2016/04/americas-army-measuring-quality-soldiers-and-quality-officers/

Goldich, Robert L., *Military Retirement and Personnel Management: Should Active Duty Military Careers Be Lengthened?* Washington, D.C.: Congressional Research Service, 95-1118F, November 14, 1995.

Grissom, Adam, "The Future of Military Innovation Studies," *Journal of Strategic Studies*, Vol. 29, No. 5, 2006, pp. 905–934.

Hall, Kimberly Curry, Kirsten M. Keller, David Schulker, Sarah Weilant, Katherine L. Kidder, and Nelson Lim, *Improving Gender Diversity in the U.S. Coast Guard: Identifying Barriers to Female Retention*, Santa Monica, Calif.: RAND Corporation, RR-2770-DHS, 2019. As of May 8, 2019:
https://www.rand.org/pubs/research_reports/RR2770.html

Huntington, Samuel, *The Soldier and the State*, Cambridge, Mass.: Harvard University Press, 1957.

Iyengar, Radha, Brad Carson, Amy Shafer, and John Winkler, "Military Power Is All About People: A Return to Military Personnel Policy," War on the Rocks, July 27, 2017. As of December 11, 2020:
https://warontherocks.com/2017/07/military-power-is-all-about-people-a-return-to-personnel-policy/

Janowitz, Morris, *The Professional Soldier: A Social and Political Portrait*, New York: The Free Press, 1971.

Kamarck, Kristy N., "Military Retirement: Background and Recent Developments," Washington, D.C.: Congressional Research Service, RL34751, 2018.

Kane, Tim, "Why Our Best Officers Are Leaving," *The Atlantic,* January/February 2011. As of March 13, 2020:
https://www.theatlantic.com/magazine/archive/2011/01/why-our-best-officers-are-leaving/308346/

Kier, Elizabeth, *Imagining War: French and British Military Doctrine Between the Wars*, Princeton, N.J.: Princeton University Press, 1997.

Klein, Katherine J., and Joann Speer Sorra, "The Challenge of Innovation Implementation," *Academy of Management Review*, Vol. 21, No. 4, October 1996, pp. 1055–1080.

Kuhn, Thomas, *The Structure of Scientific Revolutions*, Chicago: University of Chicago Press, 1962.

Lee, Caitlin, *The Culture of US Air Force Innovation: A Historical Case Study of the Predator Program*, dissertation, London: King's College War Studies Department, 2016. As of January 30, 2020:
https://kclpure.kcl.ac.uk/portal/en/theses/the-culture-of-us-air-force-innovation(b3f09298-e748-4b25-88dd-6e18f179bfde).html

Levine, Peter, "Ten Rules for Defense Management Reform," War on the Rocks, July 19, 2019. As of January 15, 2019: https://warontherocks.com/2019/07/ten-rules-for-defense-management-reform/

Lim, Nelson, Louis T. Mariano, Amy G. Cox, David Schulker, and Lawrence M. Hanser, *Improving Demographic Diversity in the U.S. Air Force Officer Corps*, Santa Monica, Calif.: RAND Corporation, RR-495-AF, 2014. As of August 21, 2019: https://www.rand.org/pubs/research_reports/RR495.html

Lindblom, Charles E., "The Science of 'Muddling Through,'" *Public Administration Review*, Vol. 19, No. 2, Spring 1959, pp. 79–88.

———, "Still Muddling, Not Yet Through," *Public Administration Review*, Vol. 39, No. 6, November–December 1979, pp. 517–526.

Locher, James, "Taking Stock of Goldwater Nichols, *Joint Forces Quarterly*, Autumn 1996. As of January 16, 2019: https://apps.dtic.mil/dtic/tr/fulltext/u2/a423058.pdf

Lundvall, Bengt-Ake, "National Systems of Innovation: Towards a Theory of Innovation and Interactive Learning," in *The Learning Economy and the Economics of Hope*, London: Pinter Publishers, 1992, pp. 85–104.

Matthews, Tim, "The US Military Doesn't Have a Problem with Brain Drain," Task and Purpose, November 16, 2015. As of March 13, 2020: https://taskandpurpose.com/the-us-military-doesnt-have-a-problem-with-brain-drain

Maucione, Scott, "Outgoing DoD Personnel Chief Says Reforms Were Inevitable, More to Come," *Federal News Network*, April 11, 2016. As of March 13, 2020: https://federalnewsnetwork.com/defense/2016/04/outgoing-dod-personnel-chief-says-reforms-inevitable-come/

———, "Is Force of the Future Back from the Dead?" *Federal News Network*, May 12, 2017. As of March 13, 2020: https://federalnewsnetwork.com/defense-news/2017/05/is-force-of-the-future-back-from-the-dead/

Mayfield, Mandy, "New Air Force Warfighting Think Tank Gets to Work," *National Defense*, January 29, 2019. As of September 29, 2019: https://www.nationaldefensemagazine.org/articles/2019/1/29/new-air-force-warfighting-think-tank-gets-to-work

McInniss, Kathleen J., *Goldwater-Nichols at 30: Defense Reform and Issues for Congress,* Washington, D.C.: Congressional Research Service, 2016.

Merriam Webster's Dictionary, s.v. "stagnant." As of March 15, 2020: https://www.merriam-webster.com/dictionary/stagnant

Military Compensation and Retirement Modernization Commission, *Report of the Military Compensation and Retirement Modernization Commission: Final Report*, 2015. As of March 13, 2020: https://docs.house.gov/meetings/AS/AS00/20150204/102859/HHRG-114-AS00-20150204-SD001.pdf

Miller, Judith, "Implementing Change," in Ash Carter and John P. White, eds., *Keeping the Edge: Managing Defense for the Future*, Cambridge, Mass.: MIT Press, 2001, pp. 285–307.

Misztal, Blaise, Jack Rametta, and Mary Farrell, "Personnel Reform Lives, But Don't Call It 'Force of the Future,'" War on the Rocks, August 9, 2018. As of March 13, 2020: https://warontherocks.com/2018/08/personnel-reform-lives-but-dont-call-it-force-of-the-future/

Murray, Williamson, "Innovation Past and Future," *Joint Forces Quarterly*, Summer 1996, pp. 51–60.

Naval Chaplaincy Service, *Presentation on Military Chaplaincy*, undated. As of April 30, 2020: https://www.churchofengland.org/sites/default/files/2018-10/gs1776-military%20chaplaincy.pdf

Nielson, Suzanne, *Preparing for War: The Dynamics of Peacetime Military Reform*, dissertation, Cambridge, Mass.: Harvard University, May 27, 2003.

Parcell, Ann D., and Amanda Kraus, *Recommendations from the CNGR Implementation Plan: Exploring the Requirements of DOPMA and ROPMA*, Alexandria, Va.: Center for Naval Analyses, CRM D0021641.A2/Final, 2010. As of April 16, 2019: https://www.cna.org/CNA_files/PDF/d0021641.a2.pdf

Public Law 96-513, Defense Officer Personnel Management Act, December 12, 1980.

Public Law 103-337, National Defense Authorization Act for Fiscal Year 1995, November 5, 1994.

Public Law 115-91, National Defense Authorization Act for Fiscal Year 2018, December 12, 2018.

Public Law 115-232, John S. McCain National Defense Authorization Act for Fiscal Year 2019, August 13, 2018.

Public Law 116-48, National Defense Authorization Act for Fiscal Year 2020, December 20, 2019.

Robbert, Albert A., Katherine L. Kidder, Caitlin Lee, Agnes Gereben Schaefer, and William H. Waggy II, *Officer Career Management: Steps Toward Modernization in the 2018 and 2019 National Defense Authorization Act*, Santa Monica, Calif.: RAND Corp, RR-2875-OSD,

2019. As of March 13, 2020:
https://www.rand.org/pubs/research_reports/RR2875.html

Robbert, Albert A., Caitlin Lee, William H. Waggy II, Katherine L. Kidder, Natasha Lander, and Agnes Gereben Schaefer, *Officer Career Management: Additional Steps Toward Modernization—Appendixes*, Santa Monica, Calif.: RAND Corporation, RR-4437/1-AF, 2021. As of January 2021:
https://www.rand.org/pubs/research_reports/RR4337.html

Robbert, Albert A., Michael G. Mattock, Beth J. Asch, John S. Crown, James Hosek, and Tara L. Terry, *Supplemental Career Paths for Air Force Pilots: A Warrant Officer Component Or an Aviation Technical Track?* Santa Monica, Calif.: RAND Corporation, RR-2617-AF, 2018. As of March 13, 2020:
https://www.rand.org/pubs/research_reports/RR2617.html

Robbert, Albert, Tara L. Terry, Alexander D. Rothenberg, Anthony Lawrence, and Neil Brian Carey, *Air Force Officer Management Flexibilities: Modeling Potential Policies*, Santa Monica, Calif.: RAND Corporation, RR-1921-AF, 2017. As of March 13, 2020:
https://www.rand.org/pubs/research_reports/RR1921.html

Rosen, Stephen P., *Winning the Next War: Innovation and the Modern Military*, Ithaca, N.Y.: Cornell University Press, 1991.

Rostker, Bernard D., *I Want You! The Evolution of the All-Volunteer Force*, Santa Monica, Calif.: RAND Corporation, MG-265-RC, 2006. As of March 13, 2020:
https://www.rand.org/pubs/monographs/MG265.html

———, "Reforming the American Military Officer Personnel System: Testimony Presented Before the Senate Armed Services Committee on December 2, 2015," Santa Monica, Calif.: RAND Corporation, CT-446, December 2015. As of April 3, 2019:
https://www.rand.org/pubs/testimonies/CT446.html

Shane, Leo, "The Pentagon's 'Force of the Future' Plan Just Got Trashed in Congress," *Military Times*, February 25, 2016. As of October 26, 2019:
https://www.militarytimes.com/news/pentagon-congress/2016/02/25/the-pentagon-s-force-of-the-future-plan-just-got-trashed-in-congress/

Simon, Herbert, *Models of Man*, New York: John Wiley, 1957.

Sisk, Richard, "Cater to Revive 'Force of the Future' Plan, Despite Lawmaker Criticism," Military.com, February 29, 2016. As of March 13, 2020:
https://www.military.com/daily-news/2016/02/29/carter-revive-forcefuture-plan-despite-lawmaker-criticism.html

Thrift Savings Plan, *Implementation of the Blended Retirement System*, Bulletin 17-U-1, April 5, 2017. As of October 29, 2019: https://www.tsp.gov/PDF/bulletins/17-u-01.html

Tilghman, Andrew, "Inside the Pentagon Personnel Feud That Has Roiled the Military's Most Senior Leaders," *Military Times*, May 15, 2016.

Toossi, Mitra, and Elka Torpey, "Older Workers: Labor Force Trends and Career Options," Bureau of Labor Statistics, May 2017. As of March 30, 2020: https://www.bls.gov/careeroutlook/2017/article/older-workers.htm

U.S. Army Human Resources Command, *Administrative Instructions for Officers Requesting to Defer Promotion Consideration (Opt Out)*, MILPER Message 19-312, Fort Knox, Ky.: U.S. Army Human Resources Command, 2019.

U.S. Code, Title 10, *Armed Forces*, 1976. As of December 16, 2019: https://www.loc.gov/collections/united-states-code/?dates=1976&fa=partof:u.s.+code:+title+10:+armed+forces

U.S. Department of Defense, *Continuation Pay Rates—2019*, Washington, D.C.: Department of Defense, January 11, 2019. As of March 30, 2020: https://militarypay.defense.gov/Portals/3/Documents/BlendedRetirementDocuments/Continuation%20Pay%20Rates%20for%202019.pdf?ver=2019-07-24-132059-003

U.S. Department of Defense, Office of Financial Readiness, *A Guide to the Uniformed Services Blended Retirement System*, December 2017. As of July 9, 2018: https://militarypay.defense.gov/Portals/3/Documents/BlendedRetirementDocuments/A%20Guide%20to%20the%20Uniformed%20Services%20BRS%20December%202017.pdf?ver=2017-12-18-140805-343

U.S. Department of Health and Human Services, Commissioned Corps of the U.S. Public Health Service, America's Health Responders, "Overview," undated. As of December 23, 2019: https://usphs.gov/questionsanswers/overview.aspx

U.S. Marine Corps Headquarters, Marine Corps Order 1001.65, *Officer Retention and Prior Service Accessions*, Washington, D.C.: Department of the Navy, December 11, 2014.

U.S. Office of Personnel Management, *General Schedule Classification and Pay*, webpage, undated. As of October 29, 2019: https://www.opm.gov/policy-data-oversight/pay-leave/pay-systems/general-schedule/

U.S. Senate, "Hearing on the Officer Personnel Act of 1947," Washington, D.C., July 16, 1947.

Vandergriff, Donald E., "Personnel Reform and Military Effectiveness," Project on Government Oversight, August 24, 2015. As of March 13, 2020: https://www.pogo.org/investigation/2015/08/personnel-reform-and-military-effectiveness/

Warner, John T., *Thinking About Military Retirement: An Analysis for the 10th QRMC*, Alexandria, Va.: Center for Naval Analyses, CRM D0017798.A1/Final, 2008. As of April 16, 2019: https://www.cna.org/CNA_files/PDF/D0017798.A1.pdf

Wilson, James Q., *Bureaucracy: What Government Agencies Do and Why They Do It*, New York: Basic Books, 1989.